Dostoevsky has written,

"The ant knows the formula of his anthill. The bee knows the formula of his beehive. They do not know their formula in a human way, but in their own way. Only man does not know his formula."

This book is dedicated . . .
. . . to the reader who is alone now and attempting to find a new formula for living Without a Man in the House. This book was written as an aid in providing such a formula.

Contents

Foreword

"Til death do us part," is a common phrase in the wedding vows. To the ecstatic young couple repeating those words, death may seem a very vague and far-off reality.

But pragmatically, nothing is more certain in the wedding ceremony than the fact that, should their marriage avoid the pitfall of divorce, someday death will take one of them and the other will be left alone.

All too quickly the honeymoon passes and the children who are born to the marriage grow up and leave home to establish homes of their own or to pursue careers in other cities. On the downswing of the cycle, the couple is back again to two plates on the table.

When they have adjusted to being a twosome once more, sooner or later (and always sooner than they anticipate) one will be incapacitated by disease or stroke, or accident and death will sever the relationship. One will be reverently buried in the family plot and the other will be kissed and comforted by family and friends and allowed to go home to find herself or himself segregated to a life alone.

Because women outlive men by almost eight years the greater percentage of persons losing mates is women.

In terms of stress, the loss of a mate registers higher than the loss of children, or parents, or wealth, or homes, or health, or any other calamity that may befall one. All other stresses occur when the victim has a mate to help bear the grief or tragedy. But now, when she or he must bear the greatest of all stresses, there is no consoling pat on the shoulder, no murmured words of comfort, no sharing. The greatest grief of all must be borne alone.

Realizing the difficulty of this adjustment which the majority of women will be called upon to bear, I have purposed to write a book which I hope may be helpful to those who read it and are "working through" their grief and making the necessary adjustments to living alone. While this book is not especially for the divorcee, the grief that she must bear is very similar to that of the widow and is sometimes more difficult for it is complicated by a feeling of rejection. I believe that she, too, may benefit from the reading. I must ask forebearance for inserting my personal experiences of these past years for, had it not been for the tragedy in my own life, I could not and would not have chosen to write these pages.

I have also drawn on the experiences of my friends and acquaintances. While the incidents related are factual, to avoid any embarrassment to these dear people I love, I have substituted fictional names.

"Working through" grief is a common expression popularized by Granger E. Westgate, a Lutheran clergyman, in his helpful book, *Good Grief,* published by Fortress Press in Philadelphia.

"Why does God permit the hurricane, when the gentle rain is so desirable?" Because it is in the deep water of the flood that our souls are forced to rely on him and become strong in the swirl of the Gethsemane experience so that we may in turn some day help someone else who is fighting the backlash of the stream, the murkiness of the tidewaters, and needing, often desperately, the understanding and help which we, through God's love, can give.

One of the common complaints made by widows is that they do not have anyone to discuss things with—no real listening ear. I still find myself delighting in some event or happening and thinking how my husband would enjoy hearing about it—only to be startled into the realization that I can no longer share my thoughts with him. Ours had been a sharing marriage—the day ending with each of us communicating to the other the events of interest that had happened. His were often student-related incidents and mine more often concerned the anecdotes of friends, children and grandchildren.

How we laughed over the tale of a friend's grandchild who had spent a morning digging worms in a garden which he made in a box in grandma's garage. "Don't you think they will be lonely for their friends?" my friend asked, hoping he would return the crawlers to their earth home. Later she was amazed to have her small Huckleberry Finn come rushing to the door, "Come, look, Grandma! I've found all their friends and now they won't be lonely anymore!" Instead of getting rid of the worms, her question had only served as a catalyst for him to bring in twice as many as he had in the first place.

The joy of any serendipity was always doubled when I shared it with my husband—and I suppose I shall always miss his explosive laughter over some trivial incident. What was a part of my day became a part of his when I shared it with him. Then, too, disappointment when shared always lost its serrated edge in the telling and in the responsive listening that he so graciously provided.

This "sharing void" is one of the most difficult to fill satisfactorily. I have found it helps to have "sharing friends." Several of my friends, themselves widows, fall into this category and it is of mutual help to exchange problems of living where we have similar interests.

The women in my weekly Bible club serve as listening posts for each other—and it helps to have a supportive group that is not bored but sympathetic when you pose problems related to plumbing, car radiators, lawn mowing, or whatever.

One word of caution here—no one will ever find your conversation as scintillating and clever as your deceased mate did. "She talks too much" can be said of far too many women. Remember: the first rule in every game of conversation is to be a good listener.

This book is written to help the widow, or divorcee, "work through" the depression of her grief by making the necessary adjustments to her new place in society as a woman alone, without a man in the house. It is the author's desire that, having read it, the reader will pass it on to someone else who has experienced or is now experiencing the great severing and needs special healing for the stub ends of her broken branches.

> You have not promised eternity to stars,
> O, God
> suns and moons will serve
> their years, disintegrate

and vanish into space.
Angels may share infinity—
I do not know—
but Your promise
for Eternal Life
is plainly given unto man:
in receiving Your salvation
we become eternal
and death is not the end
but only a link
in the chain
of Your Magnificent Circle.

1

The Other Side of the Sidewalk

For many years you have walked on the inside of the sidewalk next to glistening green lawns and the brick and stone facades of buildings. First, through your courtship years and then through the years of your marriage you were escorted by someone who loved and cherished you, who protected you from yapping dogs, from speeding cars, and noisy motorcycles that sometimes grazed the curb.

Then suddenly the great trauma that you thought happened only to other people happened to you and you found yourself walking alone on the other side of the sidewalk. You are perturbed by the nearness of the passing cars and the threat of strange dogs and stranger men.

You hug your purse tightly under your arm and, drawing yourself up to your full height, you keep your eyes straight ahead so as to avoid eye contact. Your step quickens and your heart pounds to accompany the beat of your feet. You have joined the parade of 10 million other women who also have no male escorts to protect them from the street side of life.

Already you have learned not to carry very much money with you. When you are called to walk in particularly dangerous neighborhoods to catch a train or bus, you secure your billfold with your credit cards, cash, and your driver's license on the inside of your bra where its edges press sharply against your breasts and cause you to breathe unevenly.

Restaurants are a peculiar experience. Several times you have almost walked past the cashier without paying—for you were so used to having your husband pick up the check and pay the bill. You still find it takes almost more nerve than you can summon to sit down at a table by yourself and order a meal for one. You keep your eyes lowered on your plate so as to avoid eye contact with any strange men who pass your table—just in case they have any wrong ideas.

The automobile that you used to love to ride in has become in itself a hassle. Will you ever get used to sliding into the driver's seat after years of riding beside your husband while he struggled with green and red lights, oncoming traffic and your side-seat driving? And why do gas station attendants look at you so oddly when you ask to have the oil checked or the tires tested? You don't remember noticing this down-the-nose attitude before your husband's death, but it is obvious to you now.

The airplane is another peculiar experience. You, who always had the window seat, now find yourself wedged in the center between two strange men—one of them reeking of liquor. After the introductions, you try to be distant and friendly at the same time and after a few feeble attempts at conversation, manage to glue yourself to the airline's magazine.

A concert or theater should be spelled "disaster" for

that is the label you have given the evenings when you have gone with a woman friend and marched forlornly down the aisle without the guiding hand of your husband to steer you to your reserved seat.

And church. . .when did you ever go to church alone? Not for 20 or 30 years, probably. The pews seem so strange and hard and the stained glass windows and organ music make you feel weepy. But you dare not weep in church—of all places! Do you want someone to think you have no faith? Tears are not supposed to be a part of the believer's grief—only a feeling of triumph is permitted for your beloved's entrance into the other world. Do you want people to think you are completely self-centered and concerned entirely with your own problems? Someone's words of consolation fall like cinders around you: "Praise the Lord your husband is out of this world and its trials!" You stretch your lips into a grimace and try to convince yourself that you concur.

Nothing is the same. Everything has changed. Of course, you still have your home. But home along with everything else has become a foreign land, a strange Sahara. The evenings once looked forward to are filled with weird shadows and silences. The nights are even more distressing. The headless pillow on the other side of your queen-sized bed causes the tears to gush. You prop the pillow under your own and feel some relief. Perhaps you should try sleeping in the guest room—it wouldn't hold so many memories. But no, this is your bed and you intend to prove yourself grown up now and not afraid of the dark. You intend to sleep the night in it—if it kills you—and it almost does.

And mealtime is hardly bearable. You have tried it in the kitchen and then in the dining room and both places have left you feeling insecure and gulping your food, or leaving it half eaten in order to shorten the ordeal. Will you ever get over the hollowness, the ache of missing him? Or is this something you will have to live with the rest of your life?

And weekends. You manage to push and pull yourself through the weekdays. But the weekend? How could it be that you once looked forward to them like a small child waiting up for Santa? You keep yourself extremely busy with shopping and household chores on Saturday—but Sunday, once the topping on the ice cream, is now the hardest of all days to endure. Even when you make it through church, there is yet the long afternoon that you try to fill with letter writing and TV.

Winter is especially difficult. There is something healing about being able to be out of doors in the warm spring and summer air, but to be cooped up like a Rhode Island red for the winter months and trying to get over a bereavement at the same time is all but impossible. You develop a bad case of cabin fever.

Perhaps it will help to get away from the severest part of the winter. You make plans for a stay in a Southern state—and go, reluctantly. It does help, but there is always the inevitable coming home to bare bulletin board reality. And for days after your return you find you have regressed several steps in adjusting to your new role in life. The house seems emptier than you could even remember its being. Your bedroom is especially filled with gloom. You lie down on your husband's side of the bed and, oddly, find some comfort in feeling closer to him.

My coming home this year was complicated by the fact that the water pipes were frozen. I had visions of pipes bursting all over the house and extending past the yard into the street. When the city water crew came to examine them, they told me the problem was on the "other side of the sidewalk," and when this is the case, the service is supplied by their workmen at no cost to the home owner.

"Thank You, Lord!" my heart shouted. But, there is an ugly mound on the parking lot where the men had to dig through four feet of frozen ground to free the ice. It reminds me of a grave, and every time I look at it, I think, "on the other side of the sidewalk." Yet I am grateful.

You find yourself weary because of the many responsibilities that once you shared with your husband and now are yours alone. The weight of the many details hangs over you day and night. Here, I am reminded of the domestic black woman I knew years ago who said after her husband's death, "And I just prayed, and God said, 'I will be an husband to you.'"

You are not walking on the other side of the sidewalk alone. There are hundreds of women marching with you, before you, beside you, and behind you. More important is the very real Presence there with you in the Person of our Lord and Saviour Christ Jesus. The poet Deirdre has left us a rich heritage in words that so well express the Presence of the Christ in our lives:

Christ be with me, Christ within me, Christ behind me,
Christ before me, Christ beside me, Christ to win me,
Christ to comfort and restore me,
Christ beneath me, Christ above me, Christ in quiet,
Christ in danger, Christ in hearts of all that love me,
Christ in mouth of friend and stranger.

Memorize the words and they will prove of much com-

fort to you when you feel you are walking alone on the
other side of the sidewalk. Our Lord is aware of your
struggle to make the adjustment of living without your
mate. He has reserved a very special place in his heart
for the widow and the orphan. Remember he admonished the early believers, through James, "Pure reli-
gion and undefiled before God and the Father is this, To
visit the fatherless and widows in their affliction, and to
keep himself unspotted from the world" (James 1:27).

You *can* "trust in the Lord with all your heart, and
lean not to your own understanding," and you will find
that time after time the problems that seem gigantic will
turn out to be "on the other side of the sidewalk" and
your responsibility will be relieved entirely—or greatly
diminished.

Some years ago I chose a "life verse" from the Bible.
It has proved a source of strength especially in these past
years. "For God hath not given us the spirit of fear; but
of power, and of love, and of a sound mind" (II Timothy
1:7).

When I autograph a book, I write the reference under
my name. Recently a dear woman met me after a church
service and commented on how much my poetry had
meant to her. Then she said, "But more helpful than your
poetry has been the verse you gave me when you autog-
raphed your book—I don't know how I would have gotten along without that verse of Scripture!" I am glad to
be upstaged by the Bible.

How does the Lord guide us? Yesterday, I had a strong
feeling that I should go to our farm some 50 miles away
and check on the old farm house we have been restoring
for I had not been there all winter. I was glad to find the
house just as I had left it and thanked the Lord it had not

been vandalized. The wallpaper in the dining room was still on a work table and the room half decorated. But the minute I stepped in the kitchen door, I realized something was wrong. A motor was running — and sending out a cry for help as motors often do when they are in trouble. Was it the gas furnace which had been turned to the lowest point on the thermostat, or was it the motor on the pump to the well?

Basements have always been something to avoid—and especially the very old basement in the farmhouse. Opening the basement door, I found the switch and turned the basement light on. I noticed the board my grandson had placed over a hole in the foundation had fallen to the floor. The sun came in illuminating the spot where the bricks were missing. I wondered what else had come in. . .rats. . .raccoons. . .or?

The fear I had had in the past for such creatures was completely gone. I made my way over to the furnace and found the sound was coming from what appeared to be a motor by a storage tank for water. Seeing a valve on a water line, I reached for it and turned it slowly off. It had no effect upon the running motor. Back upstairs I went outside to the well in front of the house. At that instant a car drove into the drive and I recognized the young man who lived in our trailer. *At that instant. . .*it was shortly after the noon hour and he had come home to pick up his mail. Together we discussed the problem. He took the cover from the well and we could see the water level was extremely low. The water was not seeping into the well from the ground level to about six feet below. The frozen ground was keeping the water from draining into the well!

*At that instant. . .*God is always on time. Never late

nor early. He had caused me to arrive at the farm right
when Tim came home at noon (which I did not know he
did). I was spared calling a plumber and an unnecessary
bill. More than that was the lack of fear he had given me
when it was necessary for me to explore the dark under-
ground world.

Our Lord is not only on the other side of the sidewalk—when it is necessary, he is on the underside, too.

> I must walk the other side
> of the sidewalk now, Alone.
> Where hundreds of others
> have walked before
> and shall walk after me.
>   No one takes my arm
>   at crossings.
>   No one says "stop"
>   or "you can go now"
>   when the lights turn
>   red or green.
> I must brave the yap of dog
> the swerve of car
> the grate of horn. Alone.
>   Now, the light turns yellow
>   and I remember You said
>   "I am the Light of the world"—
>   the darkness flees—
>   and I know
>   I am, can never be—alone.

2

Some Through the Flood

I could bear the days. There was always some activity in the house. The phone rang. People came to the doors. Cars on the street mirrored themselves in the windows to be reflected again from the large mirror in the dining room, or from the narrow mirror in the front hall. There was always the press of dishes to wash, groceries to put away, and the seemingly endless tasks that make a woman's day go quickly. Now mine had the added task of visiting the hospital every day to see my critically ill husband.

The nights were something else. The day sounds disappeared with the set of sun and strange noises took their places. Memories. . . Sounds of doors opening and closing, voices of the children who once ran boisterously up and down the stairs, and called to each other from the 10 rooms that had been home for so many years. I could hear the peculiar rhythm on the stairs. . .ta, ta, da. . .ta, ta, da. . .our middle child, and her father's voice calling out to her protesting the racket her feet were making. His daughters were to walk with due respect in the sanctity of their home. . .no rowdiness ever.

And the singing voices around the piano. Glad, joyful sounds that now seemed to race tauntingly around the room and then end in a groan which was usually my own, sometimes plainly audible, but often deep in the frayed fibers of my being where only my inner self could hear.

The house itself made strange noises at night. Noises I had never listened to before intruded on my silence. A window contracting in the change of the day's temperature to the cooler degrees of night. The gasp of a worn stair tread. The hollow sound of wind in the fireplace. The shifting weight of old timbers. The drip of a faucet. . .persistent. . .annoying.

I could count on my fingers the nights I had spent alone in a house before the traumatic illness of my husband. Alone. . .alone. . .I who had lived in the center of so much activity. Three teen-agers multiplied numbers of times over by their friends and their friends' friends. And my husband's students. Often they appeared at our door with their mates and children. "Just going through town and thought we would drop by. . ."

Oh, they still came but the joy and laughter which once marked their visits were gone now. They came to inquire about my husband's condition. And the repeating over and over the story of his losing bout with encephalitis, the sudden onslaught of the disease 10 days after our return from a winter in Florida, the respiratory failure, the narrow escape from death, the brain damage, the complete amnesia and the little understood aphasia was always painful. But necessary especially to his students who had loved him and had been inspired by his teaching. The prognosis? There had never been one. The doctors could make none—only God knew the course the dread disease would take and whether or not his brain would replace the damaged cells. . .whether or not his memory would return. . .and when.

The disease struck 12 days after we returned from the South where we had walked the catwalk in Highland Hammock in Sebring, and taken the boat trip on the Sewanee River—both swampy areas where mosquitoes were noticeably present. Although the virus was never to show up in the laboratory tests, the incubation period of 10 to 15 days was to fit the puzzle along with the symptoms and their devastating effects. St. Louis encephalitis, mosquito-borne and brain-crippling, could easily have been the cause.

When the disease first struck, I found myself dismayed first at my husband's paralyzed condition, and then at my own. As a child I could never understand why our pastor had always prayed for the sick and then for the persons caring for the sick. Surely the persons caring for the sick were not sick—or were they? My wise old pastor knew they were in as much need for spiritual help and prayer as were their ill loved ones. It took me 50 years to discover what he had meant. Oh, we had the usual run of childhood diseases, high temperatures, minor accidents, and health worries in rearing our children, but I did not know what "physical trauma" or "physical disaster" really meant until my physically strong husband was struck down almost overnight.

People who know me and have worked with me often comment on my easygoing nature and my ability to remain calm in a crisis, and not to get upset by unusually trying circumstances. But suddenly I found myself upset to the core of my being. The strain of the day caused me to lie awake for hours and then to fall asleep out of sheer exhaustion. I could barely get out of bed come morning. I moved as though I were treading water. Getting up was difficult. Getting dressed was equally difficult. I could care less about eating. Apathy gripped my being. I could not do my housework. Going to a grocery store was a painful experience. I was in limbo.

I was again experiencing the dizzy feeling I had over the brown stagnant water that moved lethargically under the Florida catwalk, two weeks before the trauma began. As long as there were green water lilies beneath my feet, I was all right, but when the brown swirling water took over, my stomach turned over with it and if it had not been for the steadying hand of my husband, I could easily have slipped off the walk and into the alligator infested water.

Although I had been an avid reader, reading was beyond me now except for the Psalms and some poetry. For the most part even familiar Bible passages were too heavy for my emotionally unstable mind. Newspapers became a blur before my eyes. I no longer cared what was happening in the world around me. My own private world had collapsed.

I was a stranger to myself. I was someone I no longer knew. As the days and nights dragged by with no easing of my husband's condition, I secretly wondered if I would make it — or would I break completely under the strain. Death—I might have faced it more easily, but to see my husband's fine mind destroyed was almost more than I could tolerate.

What are you doing, God? Was it all a freak of nature that could have been avoided if we had not gone out on the catwalk, or taken the boat ride on the Sewanee river.

Should my husband not have taken the cortisone prescribed earlier by our doctor for the stress hives that accompanied his retirement? The cortisone had reduced the swelling of the hives, but the one great weakness of the medication, according to our doctor, was that it lessened the body's ability to fight off disease. Was the virus-induced disease a prime example of a medicine curing one ailment and opening the door to another? I shall never know.

Praying, too, became a mystery. I swung from the extreme of wondering if I had not prayed enough for his recovery to wondering if I had prayed too long and too hard and God had "granted my request but sent leanness to my soul"—the leanness being my husband's damaged brain cells.

"Make room for mystery," my writing teacher often said. At last my restless striving for answers gave way to a place for God's mystery and the realization that there are many experiences in life to which God alone holds the answers.

I could not bear the "old familiar places." I found it necessary to go to a different church where I would not experience the agony of his not being with me.

Nor did I dare let myself go to the school where he had taught for over 30 years. When, a year after his illness, I was invited to come for a radio interview in regard to my newly published book of poetry, I forced myself to accept the invitation but wondered at the wisdom of my decision. However, God's grace was again sufficient for my need. I lived through the day in triumph and did not break once when fellow faculty members and students approached me to ask about my husband's condition.

It was the same grace that enabled me to spend long

hours of vigil beside my husband's bed and to watch the contortions of his seizures, the debilitation of the paralysis, the staggering change in his mentality without breaking into tears. It enabled me to comfort his friends who came with intentions of comforting me but broke into tears of their own. Oh, I knew the floodgate of tears — but on my knees before God, and on my pillow at night.

I am writing this from our trailer home in Florida which we purchased two months before the illness struck. It has been vacant for two years and I have come here in order to make a decision either to keep it and use it or to put it up for sale. I could not make such a decision without the proper perspective of spending time in it alone.

I awoke this morning and in my half-sleep it was two years ago. Realizing my husband's bed was empty, I thought for a moment he had gone with some of our neighbors to pick strawberries in the early morning. I listened for the mocking bird that two years ago awakened us each morning—and then the silence forced reality home: I am alone in southern Florida and two thousand miles from the nursing home where my husband has spent the past two years.

Alone. . .I can either give way to self-pity and regretful thinking and living in the past, or I can be thankful for the one wonderful winter we enjoyed in this place.

The morning we left Monet Acres to return to Wheaton, Illinois, returns in a wave of remembering. My husband was working hard to finish putting an ornamental block skirt around the trailer. He came in for a drink of orange juice and as he went back out the door, he said, "Well this is not exactly my cup of tea, but at least *you* have a place you can get out of the cold weather." That had been my doctor's orders due to a health problem I had developed.

At the time I thought the statement odd: where did he think *he* was going to be? Before I could ask him he disappeared out the trailer door to complete his work on the concrete blocks. Did he have a premonition of some kind? Was that why he was anxious to finish before we returned to Illinois?

Some persons choose winter homes in a warm clime simply because they do not like cold weather, but my husband's choice of southern Florida was because the cold weather was actually a threat to my life. "Get out of it!" my doctor told me—and get out of it we did.

Now, I find I am enjoying this place. . .this spot my husband chose for me out of his concern for my health. It is a wonderful place to escape the kill of winter, to recoup frayed nerves, to write, and to adjust to being alone.

Being here is the acid test for my aloneness. I have no telephone, no TV, no car, and my radio does not work very well. Alone. . .but I am not alone entirely. Always I am aware of the presence of our Lord. I know that He knows my needs. The RSV renders Psalm 94:19 thusly: "When the cares of my heart are many, thy consolations cheer my soul." The divine cheering of the soul is a reality here in southern Florida just as I found it to be a reality in Illinois. God's grace knows no boundaries of state or country.

Oh, not that I do not have my grief-brimmed moments. Yesterday, as I was washing dishes, an old-memory flag caught me up in its furls. In the cupboard were several of our wedding dishes, dishes I had forgotten were there, dishes that brought back a floodtide of wedding and honeymoon days. Days that were over and gone.

Three years ago, my neighbor across the street lost her husband in what should have been a routine operation for gallstones. A devout Catholic, she still has not adjusted to living alone. Again this winter, her sister has given up her position in Newfoundland and come to Florida to be with her. Living alone is a difficult adjustment some women never fully make.

While I do not think an incessant stream of busyness is advisable, complete idleness is devastating to the person who is trying to learn to cope with living alone. It is essential to find friends and activities that are of special interest. Some women find it helps to go back to work; others find volunteer work in hospitals and nursing homes especially rewarding. Some find further educational courses therapeutic. Others find a hobby such as painting, sculpting, crewel, macramé, or ceramics.

Poetry has for years afforded me a live field of interest. Since my husband's illness, I have found it of increasing importance to me in all its aspects—in the writing, reading and study of the craft.

A letter came last week from a poet friend who moved to North Carolina two years ago when her husband retired. Her letter told me he had died on Thanksgiving Day (their 48th wedding anniversary) after a long bout with cancer. He had had many operations and during his last week he was given 46 blood transfusions.

I marvelled at the letter — not one word of complaint about moving far from her friends, nor that their retirement years had been so brief. No despair about what she would do without him. Only a gratefulness that they had such a long happy life together. She stated her intention to pursue her writing more intensely and to take courses at a nearby college. Her letter exuded her joy to be alive and determination to live each day as if it were a special gift from the hand of God.

During those first several weeks of adjusting to being alone, God sent a very special help into my life. A friend invited me to visit her Bible study group every Tuesday morning. It was a small group comprised of women who had all gone, or were going, through traumatic experiences.

Hebrews was our first study book. In my Bible, I discovered in the margin of one of the first chapters these words in my husband's handwriting: "apt to think our situation the worst." Exactly. At that time I was thinking no one, but no one, had ever gone through the trauma of seeing her husband degenerate from a wise counsellor and teacher to someone with the mentality of a child.

Slowly, I realized my situation was far from being the worst. In the long days I spent in the neurological departments I saw young women with small children to rear while their hubands lay in hospital beds, mere vegetables. My husband and I had enjoyed 30-some years of happily married life, and he had completed his ministry in sacred music. Our children were married, each to a wonderful mate, and each was walking with the Lord in fields of dedicated service.

The weekly Bible study became a very important and supportive help in my life. Each of us shared our victories and our failures. We studied the Word and prayed for each other. In a short time, I came to realize that God had suited each particular problem to each person and I knew in my heart that I would not exchange problems

with any woman in the group. A divorcee and five children to rear alone? Early widowhood with three teenage
boys to guide through dating and college? A remarriage,
after several years of separation, to a self-centered husband plus worries over a daughter who had attempted
suicide? As difficult as my own cross was, it was easier
for me to bear than any of the others. I knew God had
tailor-made it especially for me and my soul's tempering
in his fire—and I also know that by his grace, I shall
come out as fine gold!

The words of the old hymn ring often in my ears: "No
never alone, no never alone. He promised never to leave
me, never to leave me alone."

For the born-again Christian there is no such thing as
being alone. God is true to His promise in the 16th chapter of John to send the Comforter—and truly the Comforter has come!

"We have no fear but fear itself!" cried Franklin
Roosevelt at the height of World War II. God does remove fear from the heart of the woman alone. "For God
hath not given us the spirit of fear; but of power, and of
love, and of a sound mind." II Timothy 1:7 is still in the
Bible—and you will find it often in these pages.

"There is nothing," we cry with Paul, "that can separate us from the love of God. . ."

> Why is it, God
> some know only gentle rain falling
> while some must know the tidal wave
> and its devastation?
>
> Why must some know the beating,
> lashing of cyclone, hurricane

and tornado
while others know only
mild trade winds blowing
and the kiss of a summer breeze?

Why do some know the warming
of sand and sun and palmetto trees
while others cringe in the blast
and sting of a long hard winter's freeze?

Why for some men are there miles of smooth
long highways and years of driving
and for others the pain, the accident
the tangled mass of steel's conniving?

You know and are the Answer—
but sometimes, being only human
sitting beneath our gourd vines
watching them shrivel, die
like Jonah by Ninevah
we wonder, then remembering

Your sovereignty
we do not ask "Why?"

3

Working Through Grief

One of the faults of intellectual Protestantism, according to Dr. Erich Lindemann, Professor of Psychiatry at Harvard, has been the misinterpretation of the passage of Scripture "Grieve not as those who have no hope. . ."

We have become bound with the precept of Stoicism which, of course, teaches that emotion is to be suppressed, stifled, and never expressed. We have not understood the difference between Stoicism and Christianity. Through both the Old Testament and New Testament, the Scripture is sympathetic to the grief stricken and recognizes the need for tears.

When my friend Margaret's husband died, no one would let her cry. The nurse who had been in attendance at her husband's death stayed on for several days and was the worst offender in this respect. If the nurse had been up to date on the findings in her profession she would have known that tears are a necessary part of the grief experience. My friend, who had been deeply devoted to her husband for 25 years, went through the funeral arrangements, the memorial, and the burial with a forced smile as a "testimony" to her faith. As is so often the case, her friends ascribed to the precept that tears were an evidence of a lack of faith. Although they were concerned and well intentioned, she could not cry in their presence.

Every Sunday school child knows the verse, "Jesus wept." Not only is it recorded that our Savior wept at the home of Mary and Martha upon learning of their brother's death, but there are many accounts of strong men of faith in both the Old and New Testament who spent hours, or sometimes a day or night, in tears. In Psalms 107:6 we read, "And they cried unto the Lord in their trouble. . ." Paul writes in Acts 20:31, "I ceased not to warn every one with tears. . ."

Fortunately, the comma has been changed in some translations of I Thessalonians 4:13 so that it reads: "Grieve, not as those who have no hope. . ." In Good News for Modern Man, the verse reads, ". . .we want you to know the truth about those who have died, so that you will not be sad, as those who have no hope." The comma makes a world of difference in the meaning. Grief is an important part of the human experience. No one escapes the experience of grief—from the grief over a smashed fender, or an unhappy "puppy love" (which is never a small thing to the puppy), to the loss by death, or other separation, of someone who was dearly loved.

However, the writer of Hebrews tells us "not to give way to apathy, but to work out our problems." Grief is one of the problems that we need to work through. A woman I shall describe more fully in another chapter kept everything complete to pipe, newspaper, and slippers just as they were the day her husband died; she had never succeeded in working through her grief experience. She had never been able to release herself from her over-preoccupation with, and bondage to, her dead mate and thereby to be free to establish herself in her world of reality.

Perhaps she had no real faith to buoy her up, and no understanding friends to help her. However, the depression of grief that accompanies the loss of a mate may be overwhelming, but it can be conquered.

There is real value in the premise that grief has stages. Dr. Lindemann wrote an article in which he demonstrated the differences between normal grief reactions and abnormal, neurotic, or morbid grief. He emphasizes the importance of helping the grief-stricken person to recognize the struggle necessary in "working through" her grief. It is necessary, he says, to "extricate oneself from the bondage to the deceased" and "find new patterns of rewarding interaction." The five stages of grief described by Dr. Lindemann are: (1) somatic grief, (2) preoccupation with the image of the deceased, (3) guilt, (4) hostile reactions, (5) and loss of patterns of conduct.

I am certain Dr. Lindemann's findings have been significant in aiding clergymen in particular to help their parishioners in "working through" grief. However, it has been my own experience that these stages of grief, while they are all a part of the grief experience, are not separate entities that come in separate chronological stages, but rather are closely inter-related. The individual is most often struggling in several or all five stages on the same muddy cross-country run. It might be simpler if one could complete one stage before starting another, but grief is not a simple experience. It is a complex matter, and working through it may prove to be the most difficult job you, or I, have ever had.

In Westgate's book, *Good Grief,* there are ten stages of grief:

1. shock or anasthesia;
2. emotional expression;
3. depression and loneliness;
4. physical distress symptoms;
5. panic and fear;
6. sense of guilt over loss;
7. hostility and resentment;
8. inability to return to normal activities;
9. hope returning;
10. struggle to reaffirm reality.

All of these various stages I am sure are present to a greater or lesser degree, depending upon the character or disposition of the individual. But again, it has been my observation that grief is not a train ride in which we pass the various stations one by one. It is more like a motor van in which all of the stages are around us and we are surrounded by compartments that have invisible walls through which we move back and forth from day to day, night to night, and moment to moment.

Recently I saw one of the women in my Bible club for the first time since the death of her husband three weeks ago. Outwardly she was smiling and well adjusted to the loss, but upon talking with her she mentioned that she had not as yet cried over the death of her husband. I realized she was still in the first stage of grief—shock. She was anesthetized and had not yet fully realized the fact of his death. While he had died after a long illness, and I knew his death bore an element of release, I also knew that one of these days she would come out of her anesthetized state and would need the comfort and understanding of her friends.

History tells us that Abraham Lincoln suffered acutely over Ann Rutledge's death. He was unable to carry on his work and withdrew from family and friends for a year after she died. From the sorrow ingrained on his face, it may be that he carried his grief burden to his grave— possibly he was unable to share it with anyone. It was considered unmanly for a man to brood over a dead love—only poets such as Edgar Allen Poe could afford such verbal expression. However, in a volume of Lincoln's published verse is a poem to Ann Rutledge, the writing of which may have given his soul much relief.

While we often think of love as being the favorite subject of the poets, actually it takes a back seat to death. More poems have been written on death than on any other subject. Perhaps this has been due to Protestant stoicism that made giving verbal expression to grief improper. At least on paper the poet could give vent to his suppressed feelings. This same suppression of feeling may have been one of the reasons the wearing of the arm band of mourning became popular. Franklin Delano Roosevelt wore such a band for a year following the death of his mother. Eleanor Roosevelt writes of her going into the bathroom and turning on the water so as to drown out the sound of her crying after the death of her seven-month old infant son.

Dr. Elizabeth Kubler-Ross, a psychiatrist on the staff of Albright's Memorial Hospital in Chicago, did a 10-year study on death and dying during which she documented the stories of persons who have been declared clinically dead and then resuscitated.

Death is often described by these persons as a long

dark tunnel or corridor through which the dying must travel. At the end is a great light. There the dying are met by friends who have preceded them in death. She attributes the light to being a religious figure "probably Jesus Christ"—who himself said, "I am the Light of the world." Not a bright glaring light that brings pain to the eyes, but a soft radiance beyond anything this world has ever known and which brings healing and joy to the beholder.

What value does such a scientific research on death and dying have for the Christian? It has merit in strengthening faith in the doctrines and beliefs that are expressed by the writers of the Bible and offers further proof as an aid to those who are left on this side of that dark corridor.

Death serves a purpose in our lives. It tends to remove the veneer from the bereaved, to make us reassess our priorities.

Psychologists refer to the "ego-person" and the "authentic-person." Our ego-persons are self-seeking and bound by false standards of materialism and in-world popularity. The authentic person is the real you that perhaps you reserve for only a few of your closest friends when the gleam of the evening gown is gone and you are in your work-around-the-kitchen gingham. Bereavement properly serves to remove the veneer of the ego-person and to permit the gentle, genuine character of the authentic-person to come into the fore. This may be one of the major reasons why bereavement is necessary to the fine growth of the soul.

"Work on your problems. . .do not give way to apathy." Nothing in this life is permanent. . .grief, too, shall pass. And joy shall come in the morning!

All winds blow out to sea:
the fetid winds of summer
licking hot tongues on field, or grove,
the frigid winds of winter
skating on frozen ponds and river beds
   The winds of April
   bathing the earth in green-Spring
   And the winds of October
   smoky from leaf-burning—
   these make the sea
   their ultimate destiny.
The hurricane, tornado
flee their destruction
for an ocean grave
   And so the tempests
   that stir heart-wave—
   these too at last give way
   to calm, failing to enslave.

4

In the Path of Trauma

Elliott Powers was a young attorney with a bright future ahead of him when he married Sara Pringle. She was a little surprised on their wedding night to receive along with his gift of a gold locket two legal documents: one was his will in which he named her as his sole heir, and the other was a power of attorney form duly filled out, signed and witnessed by a notary public. The latter consisted of four legal-sized papers, neatly encased in a blue manuscript cover.

Sara Powers at the time of her wedding might have preferred a romantic love poem declaring her bridegroom's eternal love—but in truth the papers he gave her were just that in a language that the legal world could respect and understand.

Jerry and Elizabeth Gray were in their early 50s. Their two children were in college. They looked forward to a time when they could take an early retirement from the jobs they had held for many years. Their beautiful home in the Pacific Northwest was all but paid for; they had money for their children's education and a comfortable nest egg besides. Who would dream that a bout with Asiatic flu could completely upset their lives? Jerry didn't seem to be getting over the two weeks he spent in bed. In fact, when he got up for meals or to go to the bathroom, he lost his equilibrium and fell. A long series of hospital tests failed to reveal the problem, but the falls continued. Then came memory loss and speech problems. The medical insurance ran out but the stupendous bills increased. Their savings dwindled and disappeared. Elizabeth, burdened by his illness, struggled to keep her children in college. Finally it became necessary to have Jerry declared mentally incompetent, placed in a mental institution, and to endure the hassles and added expense of a conservatorship.

Doctors in the sanitarium became interested in Jerry's case. "He doesn't belong here," they said. "He needs an operation on his brain—a pocket of infection caused by a virus." Elizabeth found herself in a legal hassle with state authorities in order to get her husband released. The operation was successful, but it left some paralysis on the left side—and months and years of emotional and financial stress on the family.

While the disease and its consequences were unavoidable, much of the expensive legal harrassment would not have happened had the Grays given each other power of attorney papers early in their marriage.

"Nothing like that could ever happen to me" is what most people tell themselves. But it could, today, in an auto accident, or as commonly, a fall in the familiar surroundings of the home.

Fred Murfin was a roofing contractor. He often climbed the ladders and helped his men finish a job. An early frost made the roof slippery and he fell 16 feet to disaster. Concussion and a brain clot resulted in paralysis and complete aphasia. His wife was faced with horrendous business problems—many of which could have been more easily resolved had she had in her lock box, along with the deed to their home and other important papers, a simple power of attorney.

The Stovers owned a real estate business. Although small in size, it was doing quite well despite the decline in sales in the suburb in which they operated. When her husband complained of headaches that aspirin did not seem to alleviate, Mary Stover made a doctor's appointment for him. The encephalogram revealed problems that were localized in a small tumor. An operation followed which proved the tumor to be benign, but the neurosurgeon was blunt in his prognosis: "Chances are it will grow back within the next few months or years." Fortunately for the Stovers, Mike Stover's aphasia did not last long and there is still time for them to take care of legal matters where their business is concerned. But will someone impress upon them the importance of having power of attorney forms made out before he is threatened by further surgery?

Much is written about keeping your will up to date, but very little appears in print about the importance of power of attorney papers. The form is so simple in fact it is not necessary to have a lawyer—but it is necessary to have it properly signed before a notary public before the accident or illness that brings about mental disturbances.

Many men, otherwise thoughtful and considerate of their families, fail to make out a will — even Peter Marshall died intestate. This means unnecessary costs of probate court procedures when death occurs.

To the average person, power of attorney means some

form or other made out in order to accomplish a specific purpose or a one-time legal action through a bank, trust or other institution. Few persons realize that a power of attorney can prove to be a safeguard against legal and financial red tape should an accident or illness result in mental incompetence.

During the weeks of my husband's hospitalization, I became acquainted with Miriam Underwood. The Underwoods had retired three years ago and moved to the Ozarks where they built their dream home and settled down to the simple joys of garden clubs, fishing and county fairs. One morning Jim Underwood stumbled out of bed with a stabbing pain in his left eye. He had had a similar pain some years before and recognized it as a detached retina. Since the nearest eye doctor was a hundred miles away, the Underwoods decided to return to their former home and enter the eye clinic which had served them in the past.

Miriam threw a change of clothing into her handbag and thought she would be away from home for a night or two. Jim came no better prepared for the ordeal that lay before them. Upon examination, the eye doctor phoned the hospital to have him admitted for more complete examination facilities. The X-rays showed a brain tumor which was further complicated by other tumors that were evidenced in his lung X-rays. As we sat together in the lunchroom, Miriam Underwood confided her fears to me. Her husband had always managed all of the business affairs. Her name wasn't even on their bank accounts. She had married right out of high school and had had no business experience whatever. She knew that if he were to come out of the operation a mental cripple she wouldn't even be able to write a check to pay one bill.

The Underwoods were forced to take a furnished apartment near the hospital where Miriam could walk back and forth because she had never learned to drive a car. No one knew when they would be able to return to their home in the Ozarks. She had called a neighbor asking her to pack some of her clothing and ship it to her.

I suggested to her that she open a checking account in a nearby bank and have their trust department make out both a simple will and a power of attorney form. She lost no time taking care of that, and when I saw her at lunch the next day, she showed the forms to me, which her husband had signed before witnesses and a notary public from the hospital staff. I never knew the outcome of the operation, or how long Jim Underwood lived (the doctors had said his case was terminal) but I did have the satisfaction of knowing his widow had been legally protected by the two simple documents she had obtained and had him sign before his serious surgery.

Great numbers of persons do not have any forewarning of physical trauma, and unless their legal affairs are in good order much unnecessary hardship can be inflicted on their families.

"Why do you include such information in your book?" you may ask. "Isn't it like locking the barn after the horse has been stolen?"

The intention is to help the reader see that her legal affairs are in order before the emergency arises. The power of attorney form on the following pages is adapted from the form the young attorney gave his bride on their wedding night.

It may be too late to help you solve any of your legal problems where your late husband is concerned, but you still have legal obligations to see that your own will is in order. That is, unless you want the state to step in upon your death.

It is important that you have a proper will made out, or have your will brought up to date when your husband is gone. It is also important that you have *power of attorney* forms made out naming one of your children to carry out your business affairs in case some debilitating illness would make it impossible for you to conduct your business. Putting these matters in their proper order will give you a certain peace of mind—which is most essential to the woman living alone.

If you have no direct descendants, and no close blood relatives whom you care to remember in your will, then choose a sound Christian organization to name as your legal heir. Often such organizations have men in their legal departments who can advise you on setting up a trust or an annuity that would give you the benefit of present income and the knowledge that your assets would be left to further the cause of Christ upon your demise.

Another important instrument to have among your papers is the *LIVING WILL,* a copy of which I am including. This simply states that should you become seriously incapacitated you prefer to have death take its natural course and want no extreme emergency measures to keep you alive. This may be a grim subject to consider, but forethought can spare your loved ones much agony.*

---

*When my father-in-law suffered a stroke at 88 and was rushed by ambulance to the emergency room of the hospital, the doctor explained that along with the possibility of brain damage from the stroke, he had pneumonia. He asked us whether we wanted him to perform "Emergency 99," attempting to prolong his life, or to permit him to die a natural death. The burden of the choice was on us and it would have been much simpler had my father-in-law expressed his desire in a Living Will.

In case you would like to will your eyes, or other parts of your body, to medical science, there are cards available for this purpose. Death loses much of its power over us when we face it squarely and courageously ahead of time. Doing our "homework" before class builds confidence about meeting the appointed hour.

POWER OF ATTORNEY

BE IT HEREBY KNOWN THAT I, the undersigned_____a citizen of and domiciled at_____, do appoint my_____, of _____to serve as my true and lawful attorney for me, and in my name:

1. To make deposits, to endorse checks, promissory notes, and to make deposits in any and all accounts, both savings and checking in any bank in which I have any such account.

2. To withdraw funds from any of such checking accounts and savings by check or withdrawal drafts.

3. To have access to any safe deposit boxes which I may rent or which are now rented in my name in any bank in the United States.

4. To accept, endorse, cash, deposit any and all pension checks coming to me from any source whatsoever.

5. To enter and take possession of any lands, buildings that may belong to me.

6. To collect and receive any rents, profits of any and all such lands, or part of such lands.

7. To pay all sums of money that may be hereafter owned by me in whatever just claims.

8. To execute and perform any act, deed, matter or thing whatsoever that ought to be done in relation to

any and all property owned by me in my best interests.

In the event my said attorney-in-fact shall die or become incapable of acting as my attorney-in-fact, I hereby appoint my_____of_____to be my attorney-in-fact in place of_____, with power to exercise all or any of the powers and authorities hereinbefore conferred on said_____.

And I, the said_____, do hereby ratify and confirm all whatsoever my said attorney shall do, or cause to be done, in or about the premises, by virtue of this Power of Attorney.

IN WITNESS WHEREOF, I have hereunto set my hand and seal at_____on this_____day of_____.

Signed, sealed and delivered
in the presence of:
_____ Witness
_____ Witness

MY LIVING WILL

To my family, my physician, my lawyer, my clergyman, any medical facility in whose care I happen to be, and to any individual who may become responsible for my health, welfare or affairs:

Death is as much a reality as birth, growth, maturity and old age. It is the one certainty of life. If the time comes when I_____, can no longer take part in decisions for my own future, let this statement stand as an expression of my wishes while I am still of sound mind.

If the situation should arise in which there is no reasonable expectation of my recovery from physical or mental disability, I request that I be allowed to die with dignity. Because of my faith in Jesus Christ as my personal Savior, I do not fear death itself. But, I do fear the indignities of deterioration, dependence, and hopeless pain. I therefore ask that medication be mercifully administered to me to alleviate suffering, but that I not be kept alive by artificial means or "heroic measures."

This request is made after careful consideration. I hope you who care for me will feel morally bound to follow its mandate. I recognize this appears to place a heavy responsibility upon you, but it is with the intention of relieving you of such responsibility and of placing it upon myself in accordance with my strong convictions that this statement is made.

A simple Memorial Service could take the place of the customary Funeral Service.

Date:_____   Signed:_____

Witness:_____
Witness:_____
Subscribed and sworn to before me
this 5th day of November, 1977

_____

  Notary

  The above copy of the Living Will was given to me by a friend who keeps copies of it in her personal file. Many Christians have such documents, or similar ones, in their safety deposit boxes along with their legal Wills. Such a document does make it easier for the family, faced with the death of a loved one and the desire of the doctors to place the dying person on intravenous tubes and a respiratory machine.

But since a Living Will is part of indirect euthanasia, it is somewhat undesirable. One major problem concerns malpractice suits. Some doctors are reluctant to serve patients who show them Living Wills for fear they could be involved in legal prosecution should the patient die.

Here as in many problems in life the Holy Spirit's leading is paramount. When my husband's condition worsened, the head nurse in the nursing home showed me a paper which I could sign requesting there be "no heroics" when death threatened. For some unexplainable reason, I could not sign the paper although I knew in my heart I would not permit him—with his damaged brain—to be placed on a respirator again. I would ask that he, like his father, be permitted to "die with dignity." At the last, I preferred to say it to the nurse and doctor rather than having a signed document. In summary, this is a very sensitive matter, one in which the Holy Spirit must be in charge.

5

Aloneness or Loneliness?

"I am so very lonely," a middle-aged man confided to me recently. It had been two years since his wife died and no one could fill the void she had filled in his life. His teenaged daughter still lived at home but she had her own interests, her friends, and her school activities.

Loneliness is the greatest problem of widowhood. To lose the close comradeship that is unique to a happy marriage cannot be compared with any other loss suffered in this life.

"I just cannot go *alone*. . .it is just no fun when you have to go *alone*. . ." Or the question, "What can I do, where can I go when I am alone?"

How often we hear these remarks from the newly widowed, always with an emphasis on the word "alone." There is a vast difference between "loneliness" and "aloneness." It is a difference that cannot be fathomed immediately by the newly widowed. It must be learned gradually and with much effort of mind and soul.

Loneliness carries with it such a feeling of displacement. You may have thought of a "displaced person" as someone who has escaped from, or been expelled from, his native country. Before my husband's illness, I never realized you could be a D.P. right in your own home. And yet, when you become a woman alone, without a husband, there is no other idiom in the English language that so well describes the way you feel about yourself and the way other people feel about you.

One of the stages of grief recognized by psychologists is anger and resentment. This may be so deeply buried within you that you cannot even recognize the feeling, let alone admit it to someone else.

If you are a Christian, you can share these hidden feelings with your Lord. You are free to cry out "Forgive me Lord for these strange feelings that are seething within me. Hide them at the foot of your cross and give me your peace within, your peace that comes from accepting what you have permitted to come into my life."

In going through some papers the other day, I came across a little tract, "This Thing Is From Me," written many years ago by an Irish girl named Laura A. Barter Snow. The tract contains a reference to I Kings 12:24 where God told the prophet Shemaiah to give this message to Rehoboam and to all the people of the tribes of Judah and Benjamin: "Do not attack your own brothers, the people of Israel. Go home, all of you. What has happened is my will" (Good News translation).

The Reverend C. A. Fox added, "Life's disappointments are veiled Love's appointments." This is what your new status as a widow is — "Love's appointment."

All that concerns you concerns God, too. "He that toucheth you toucheth the apple of his eye." (Zechariah 2:8) In Isaiah 43:4 it says: "You are precious in My sight."

You are now entering a new phase of your life, one that can be very rich and full of divine blessings if you will permit it to be. We have a God who can turn tragedy into triumph. That is his business.

In the little Irish tract we read from Exodus 18:18, "This thing is too heavy for thee; thou art not able to perform it thyself alone." "You are only an instrument, not an agent," the author explains. I might add: "an instrument that is meant for the Master's use."

I have another little tract called "God Uses Those Who Are Broken." This reference is from Psalms 51:17, "The sacrifices of God are a broken spirit." The displaced person has gone through the breaking of home ties, family ties, and his or her spirit. When Gideon's soldiers broke their pitchers, then the light could shine forth to the consternation of their enemies. When we bring our broken spirits to God, we can be sure he will not destroy them for he has written in his word, "the bruised reed I will not break."

The plans you made so carefully for life with your husband are broken now, and whatever the future holds you think will be only second best. But God has a way of making second bests superior to what you may have envisioned as a first in your life. He is trustworthy and will not let you down.

Many people are working in "second best" occupational choices. My husband came to Chicago to study to be a commercial artist but the door closed to his education at the art institute and he found himself majoring in musical education. This led him to a long life of service as director of the Sacred Music Department at Moody Bible Institute. It was a position he loved because it afforded so many opportunities to help, inspire, and instruct young people — thousands of them through the 32 years he was there. His first choice never could have brought the fulfillment and opportunities for service that his second choice did.

When you are feeling like a D.P. remember D.P. also stands for "Divine Providence" or "Dedicated Promise." Oh, you have been displaced from the shelter your husband provided for so many years, but now you can know more closely the fellowship of the "Man who is like the shadow of a rock in a weary land," about whom Isaiah writes.

Although you may be displaced from all that you have known in life you can never be displaced from the Saviour who holds you securely in the palm of His hand.

Loneliness cannot be overcome by inactivity. It calls for action. Get out and meet people. "But I have never been a joiner." Become one. Your local hospitals and nursing homes are always in need of "pink" or "gray" ladies to help in their auxillaries.

Are you good at crafts? Keep your hands busy as you sit by the TV. Make stuffed mice, decorative Christmas tree ornaments, crewel owls, partridges from pear trees, or corn husk dolls for your local Family Service, hospital, or child care bazaars.

A history club is an organization, usually focusing upon the local area, that provides much interest for the woman in need of developing outside interests. Organizations like the League of Women Voters are always looking for women who want to be involved in the political scene and you may perhaps have the bloodline to qualify for membership in something like the Daughters of the American Revolution.

In her book, *Open Heart Open Home,* Karen Burton Mains points out that to show hospitality is not a choice — it's a direct command from God. True hospitality is a ministry that can bless not only the guest in your home but you as well, when you let yourself be the instrument through which the Holy Spirit blesses. Free yourself from the "entertaining trauma" fostered on us by a secular culture, and open your heart and home to the person God lays upon your heart. I cannot think of a better cure for loneliness.

The worst form of loneliness is not experienced by the widow. It is the loneliness of the wife who is married to a man who destroys her by his cold indifference or negative criticism. You have seen such marriages and wondered how on earth the wife can put up with it. Well, sometimes she doesn't. Our mental institutions are overcrowded with women (and men, too) who have been unable to overcome this form of loneliness.

Loneliness thrives on an unforgiving spirit. Are there areas in your life where you have never really practiced forgiveness? Is there someone in your past or present whom you still have grudges against? "Never let the sun go down upon your wrath." What a simple rule from Proverbs to live by — but how vital in the preservation of any human relationship. I remember the first argument I had with my husband. It was over a mere trifle and the subject I have forgotten. But my cold, sullen attitude is one I remember after 30 years. My husband gave me that verse in Proverbs and we went to bed with no ill feelings between us.

It is the course of least resistance to let your life become a path between your TV, table, refrigerator, nearby store, and bed. It takes effort to make yourself into an interesting person. If you do nothing to make and keep friends they will drop away one by one like pearls on a broken strand of beads.

The motto you learned when you were a Girl Scout should still be yours: "Make new friends, but keep the old. One is silver, and the other gold." Don't let the wood and stubble take over in your life. Keep your best silver polished and ready for spur-of-the-moment company.

In my mobile court in Florida I found delight in making small stained glass designs from plastic beads which we baked in our ovens. I described the experience like this:

> We sat in Lois's kitchen last night
> making stained glass windows
> small in size
> for the churches of our eyes.
> No sanctuary shall contain
> the windows we have made —
> no elders would permit them —
> the glasses red and blue with compromise
> were for the churches of our eyes.
>
> A cat in plastic calico
> pink of face and red of body
> a turtle in green and blue
> with one red eye, and a planter
> of yellow, brown, and avocado —
> "to hold a candle's warmth
> instead," so Lois said.
>
> With no elders there to rue
> our choices, challenge, misconstrue —
> it is amazing
> what color satisfies
> the churches of our eyes.

We daily need satisfaction for the churches of our eyes. Often these small needs are simple like birds coming to a bird feeder. How lovely it is to hear the song of sparrows especially in winter, or to see the chickadees with their trim gray and black coats hopping cheerfully about in the snow. The sudden appearance of a red bird is like a love letter dropped from heaven.

What do birds have to do with loneliness? A lot. They are small examples of how reaching out into God's world can help to overcome the feeling of desertion that is really what loneliness is.

God has not deserted you. "His eye is on the sparrow" and you can know he watches you. Even the "hairs of your head are numbered" and no matter how infinitesimally small we may feel we are, the God of the mustard seed is still in control. There is no variation, nor shadow of turning in him. He is the same yesterday, today, and forever.

6

Much Ado About Money

The greater percentage of the money in these United States is controlled by women. These are women who have, for the most part, inherited estates from their husbands or families and are untrained in money management. Overnight they are forced to adjust to complicated terminology and the legal maze that is the world of finance.

They must learn the new world of business management for they have suddenly become a part of it. But here it is well to insert a word of advice and caution: Make no hasty decisions. Sign no papers without due consideration by someone who is well acquainted with the business world. Lawyers can prove helpful, but sadly, they can also prove to be leeches out to bleed you of your life savings. Likewise, some so-called "Christian lawyers" hide under the framework of the church in order to further their own interests and lechery. These are those of whom the Scripture cried: "Woe unto them who devour widow's houses!"

Often a small-town lawyer is to be preferred, because

his reputation is important to him and the local people know him. Because of his lower overhead his fees are more modest. A woman I know had a small-town lawyer make out a will to replace one she had had made in Chicago. The small-town attorney's fee was $50; the Chicago law firm had charged her $500 for the same service.

There are also legal services available through such agencies as the Internal Revenue Service, the Federal and State Inheritance Departments, and the State Attorney's office. Don't be afraid to ask questions. Remember, your taxes are paying their salaries.

The stack of legal forms plus Medicare and Blue Cross/Blue Shield, major medical and other hospitalization and insurance papers may at first glance seem overwhelming. But you have to deal with only one form at a time and this you will learn to do.

Your public library, or post office, has a copy machine that can be of special service to you now as you mail forms to various organizations. You should keep photostatic copies in your files for each form you mail.

When Ruth Hartmann was widowed, she found herself responsible for several properties, rentals which her husband had bought for the purpose of keeping busy in his retirement. He believed in real estate as a good investment, and fortunately for her his holdings have shown fine appreciation. When and if she decides to liquidate she stands to realize very good prices. In the meantime, she has the headache of finding and keeping good renters and seeing that her houses and buildings are properly maintained.

It is wise for the new widow to continue with the investments her husband has made rather than to buy and sell on the advice of well-meaning friends. It takes an expert to succeed in the stock market, and even the experts have seen their stock holdings dwindle in paper value in recent years. Mutuals have been a good investment in the past (especially where a tax shelter was desired) but even these have proved to be less dependable than in former years.

Paul Erdman, former Swiss banker and author of *The Crash of '79,* recently expressed his disillusionment with the stock market. He advocates strong caution in investments in stocks and feels that money placed in certificates of deposit, with four- or six-year limits, is one of the soundest investments, and in real estate because real estate prices rise with inflation.

Certificates of deposit in federally insured banks is an easy no-worry, no gamble form of investment. They are presently paying interest at 7, 7½, or 8¼ percent. When the interest is left to accrue, the rate also increases. Savings and loan companies usually pay a fraction of a percent higher than banks do.

There are investments that bring a higher rate of return, but none that is surer and less troublesome than the certificate of deposit. United States Treasury bills are another good form of investment, but the minimal purchase amount is now $10,000. These must be purchased through a bank with a fee paid for the bank transaction, and, of course, the paper must be kept securely in a safe deposit box.

Investing in Mutual Real Estate Investors is a good way to take advantage of inflation savings in real estate when you do not have the know-how needed to buy and sell property. Such organizations invest your money for you and you have the advantage of their expertise. At present such MRI companies are paying good interest rates, sometimes as high as 10 or 12 percent. But here again there is far more risk involved than the dependable certificates of deposit offered by banks and/or savings and loans.

If you have never had a checking account in your own name, now is the time to establish one, preferably in the bank where you have your savings account. Pay all bills and all purchases by check. In this way an accurate record is maintained on all expenses which is most valuable in making out your income tax return. This must be done by April 15 each year.

Prudence must be exercised in keeping a sufficient amount in your checking account to cover monthly expenses. But interest is not paid on checking accounts, and so any excess should be transferred to your savings regularly. Then, when you have an additional sum of perhaps $1,000 saved over the amount in your emergency savings account it is good business to transfer this amount over to a certificate of deposit account either in your bank or savings and loan.

The use of a credit card for gasoline is a help also when making out income taxes. It is simple to figure out how many gallons have been purchased and how much of it was on taxes.

Donations to churches and charitable organizations should be paid by check in order to keep a record for tax reporting. It is equally important to pay all medical and prescription bills by check in order that you may have an accurate record of these tax-deductible costs.

Keep and file all receipts for utilities, rents, taxes, insurance, and other household expenses in order to be able to give proof of payment if payment is ever questioned. In this computerized age it is not at all unusual to be billed twice for the same service. Or, should you want to sell your home, proper receipts make it easy to tell prospective buyers what they can expect to pay in taxes, heating, and electricity.

The single woman must remember that while the total sum of her husband's estate may seem impressive she must make it last over the remainder of her life. She no longer has the steady income her husband provided and therefore cannot afford to spend as liberally as she may think she can.

Upon her husband's death, Martha Reed came into an insurance claim for $100,000. It seemed a fabulous sum to her after years of making-do on her husband's weekly take-home pay. In truth it wasn't much when she considered that it was a substitute for his earnings over the next twenty years. This, actually, allowed her $5,000 per year.

But Martha suffered from nouveau-riche pangs and gave generous sums of money for education and travel to her two sons. One day she awoke to find her capital was dwindling away. Fortunately she was able to find employment which gives her an income as well as another way of saving up money for the rainy day of her old age.

Do you think you may have 20 years to live? Then divide your net worth by 20 and see if it does not appear to you to be smaller than what you first thought. Budget your income from social security, pension, and interest on investments, or rents and royalties. As much as possible, let your capital remain untouched, even growing from interest and occasional additions. You do not know what your needs may be in the days ahead.

Let frugality become a very real part of your thinking vocabulary. Remember the word is frugality and not miserliness. There is a vast difference. You can be generous to your children, your church, and your favorite charities but avoid being foolishly generous.

Frugality is not a characteristic of the poor alone. More often it is part and parcel of the well-heeled. They have learned to respect money and never to throw it around ruthlessly in unwise, unnecessary spending. In my neighborhood are several retired farmers — men to whom capital is a very important tool. Although their land holdings could put them on millionaires' row they have made frugality a way of life.

Before I make a purchase, I often ask one of them where I can get the best buy, and invariably he knows.

The multi-millionaire John D. Rockefeller was known for his gifts of bright, shiny dimes. He was trying to impress the recipient with the importance of frugality. Little thin dimes add up to big fat dollars and earn dollars and dimes in interest when wisely invested.

The Bible cautions that "the love of money is the root of all evil," yet we are now responsible for ours. We must bring our finances before the Lord and ask for His wisdom and guidance in all of our money dealings.

You as a widow are vulnerable. Vulnerable to many unscrupulous persons who have plots and schemes to get your money. You may also find yourself vulnerable to very fine persons wanting donations for very good causes. Here is where prayer for discernment is necessary. If you were to give to all the appeals that come in your mail, you would soon be penniless and needing to appeal for funds yourself! One wise widow, who was left a large estate by her husband, and finds endless appeals in her mailbox, makes it a rule never to give money in response to an appeal unless she has had time to be alone and pray about it. This has protected her from impulse-giving.

When tempted to be overly generous with your children, you should be just as careful. It is important to remember they have several real assets you no longer have: youth, health, and the ability to earn money for themselves.

It is a real temptation to try to help them in their struggling years, but do not forget you and your husband lived through those years too. Struggle is an important ingredient in character-building. Living through those years made you all the stronger for the experience, so do not attempt to cushion your children's lives with the money your husband left. That money was meant to provide for you and your needs first. Upon your death, your children will come into their rightful share of all that remains.

The government has recently changed the gift tax limit to $3,000 a year and some parents with good-sized estates make use of this provision in order to avoid heavy gift taxes at death. Your use of the provision depends upon the size of your estate and should only be exercised after your own needs have been determined.

As soon after your husband's death as you can conveniently manage, make a visit to your local Social Security office. Take with you your husband's death certificate and file a claim for his death benefit. Also review his and your social security status. Although his monthly social security check will no longer be forthcoming, you, as his widow, may find it beneficial to file for your "widow" social security rather than that based upon your own earnings. This may make a difference of a hundred dollars or so a month. It is, unfortunately, a benefit little understood and often unclaimed by the general public.

You will need to check on how much you are permitted under federal law to earn each year and still receive your social security check. At the present time, this amount is $4800 a year. Legislation is being prepared to raise this figure, and perhaps do away with the limit entirely.

Recent statistics show that only two out of 100 persons are able to support themselves at age 65 and after. Twenty-three need the help of family and friends to meet their monthly bills. The other 75 are on public aid.

Where do you fit in these figures? Or where will you fit?

Poor Richard was not so poor after all for he knew that "a penny saved is a penny earned." Become a reader of financial columns in local newspapers and keep current on the national and international financial picture by subscribing to one of the current news magazines. Such knowledge may never make you rich, but it will keep money in your sugar bowl.

Pay bills on time and save the penalty for late payment. Take advantage of garage sales and department store sales. Acquaint yourself with the nearest resale shops. Learn to enjoy a bargain.

Take inventory of your household furnishings and possessions. It is true, as someone has said, that "we spend the first 40 years of our lives collecting things and the last 40 years giving them away." Perhaps you do need to get rid of that child's blue willow tea set ("made in occupied Japan"). Sell it, or better still give it to your own grandchild.

Will you ever again have occasion to do formal entertaining on the scale that calls for hand-painted china? If not, simplify your lifestyle to go along with your reduced level of energy. This is why mobile home living is so popular among retirees. Needs are reduced to a bare minimum. One set of dishes is all you have room for.

Learn to use credit cards, but use them with caution. Command them; don't let them command you. Many a person spending lavishly through the use of credit cards has ended up in financial ruin. When and if you do employ credit cards for purchases or travel accommodations, pay the charges each month so you will not carry a running balance and be subject to that whopping 18 percent interest charge. Keep your credit cards down to a minimum, and if one is lost or stolen report it both by telephone and in writing immediately to your creditors so you will not be held responsible for more than the customary $50 loss on each card.

David rejoiced in the fact that the gold and silver belong to God. This can be your joy also. Dedicate your possessions to him—the cattle on a thousand hills and the antiques in your cupboard. Let him grant you wisdom in what you should do with your possessions. Is there a struggling church somewhere? Or a missionary needing your assistance? Or a student having a hard time getting through seminary?

Money carries with it responsibility. Learn to use your money wisely and to be a steward accountable to the Lord.

Frugality, prudence in giving, avoidance of foolish generosity have been the theme of this chapter — but it is still very true that "you cannot take it with you. . .except for what you give away!" It is in the giving that we need the guidance and direction of the Holy Spirit.

7

Special Services
for Widows

Special Organization Services (SOS) was started by
Bill Walker, a Texas insurance agent, to provide free
help for widows and widowers who need to make sense
of the financial mess their spouses may have left behind.
So far he has sold the program to more than 900 banks
and savings and loan companies which use it as a good
will service to attract customers. A letter to SOS, P.O.
Box SOS, Athens, Texas 75751 will provide you with a
list of participating institutions in your area.

SOS counselors get two days of training on how to
track down possible sources of income, plus a detailed
manual on springing money from insurance companies,
Social Security, the Railroad Retirement Fund, teachers'
and ministers' associations, foreign insurance funds and
scores of other places that might owe the widow money.

If you are one of those women who knew very little,
even nothing, about her husband's business matters, this
sort of service might be for you. But take heart, you are
not alone. Thousands of widows each year find themselves overwhelmed by the lack of knowledge they have

about their husband's business. Some don't even know what insurance their husbands carried, the amount they have coming in benefits, or the names of the companies carrying the policies.

The apparent reluctance of husbands to keep their wives abreast of family business matters is regrettable but it may not indicate his lack of love and concern. Men, especially business executives, are often so completely involved with the business world during the day at work that when they can escape to the sanctuary of wife and children they do not want to bring these business details across the threshold of their homes with them. They are looking for diversion and escape, and this is what you may have meant in your husband's life.

This is why many a widow, after her husband's funeral, appears at her bank's door distraught, with pitiful knowledge of her husband's financial affairs.

It may have proven impossible for her to discuss such problems with friends and family, for as Bill Walker says, "In some areas, it is often considered out of place for a widow to talk about money."

One widow reportedly found an insurance policy her husband's parents had bought for him in 1908 and was about to discard it. Fortunately she took it to an SOS counselor and found it was worth $3,000. SOS is on record for finding as much as $72,000 in benefits one widow was utterly unaware of having.

Often SOS can turn up insurance on cars or on homes that are responsible for saving thousands of dollars for the widow — insurance on mortgages her husband had never mentioned having. Credit insurance often accompanies a mortgage loan.

Sometimes women do not know they are eligible for

social security for their children upon their husband's death. Often this amounts to several hundred dollars a month.

SOS supplies forms to be filled out before a man dies so that his wife will know where each asset may be found. Having such a list can save the widow much anguish of soul. When you go to an SOS counsellor pick up several forms for your friends who can take advantage of this pre-death service.

You have probably found by this time that the state moves in to seal all lock boxes in the deceased's name. A listing of all contents is made and you may have been, or may be, called in to witness the audit of the box. It is wise to be present when such an audit is made.

Sometimes a widow will rush to the bank before the bank has been notified of the death, and remove any and all contents from the box. This is unwise because there will be a record kept of the date and time you entered the box and you may find yourself suspect and required to return the contents.

SOS also offers financial counselling — helping the widow figure out how much she'll need to live on and how much she can save. The service is free and the widow is not even expected to place her money in the bank through which she has obtained the services of the Special Organization Services counsellor.

Some states are without adequate legislation to protect women's rights. For example, in Missouri a husband can, without notifying his wife, decide not to provide survivor's equity for her in his pension plan in order to collect larger pension payments while he is alive. In some states the legal position of a woman deteriorates when she marries. For example, in Louisiana, when a woman marries, her husband is declared "head and master" of all property the couple hold together; he can sell or mortgage that property without her knowledge or consent.

The International Women's Year Commission has had booklets, "The Legal Status of Homemakers," prepared which cover all of the states and most of the territories. The booklets deal with the rights of all women, both full-time homemakers, and those with outside jobs — during marriage, at widowhood, and during and after divorce. These may be obtained for a nominal price by writing to: Superintendent of Documents, U.S. Government Printing Office, Washington, D.C. 20402; or by calling the International Women's Year Commission Information Office at (202) 632-8978.

8

When Depression Rears its Hooded Head

You have been doing beautifully. Your friends tell you they admire you for your courage and bravery in the face of such a great loss, and you believe them—almost. And then today you get up as usual from a night's rest with plans for the day on your mind, and suddenly, without any warning, you are besieged with a deep depression.

What has triggered it? Maybe nothing you can identify. Or, maybe it was the notice for his driver's license renewal that came in the mail. Perhaps it was the National Geographic you found in the drawer of his bed table. You are overwhelmed by the remembrance of how he loved to read the well-illustrated pages and the way he called you over to see a special picture that impressed him, or told you to be sure to read such and such an article.

Suddenly the torrent is set free. Tears gush down your cheeks in volumes you wouldn't have believed possible. You have never been a weepy woman. But now, let yourself cry. Grief is like that: it wells up inside almost unnoticed, then something triggers the floodgate and the scalding lava comes rushing, demanding to be set free.

Fortunately, there is no one around to tell you not to cry. How often people, well-meaning in every intention, will attempt to keep a grieving person from crying. Crying is necessary. It releases the pent-up tensions, the stalemate of despair. It acts as a guard for the nerves, and a preventive against future emotional illness. Tears are in themselves healing.

Now that the torrent has ended, take a good warm shower and dress yourself in one of your favorite outfits, preferably bright in color. If it is feasible, go some place—the library, the art or history museum, the arboretum. Call a friend to go with you or to join you for lunch.

Or, go window shopping. In the past I have counted this an extravagance I could not justify wasting time on, but I find it a great help when one is trying to live with grief. One friend I know goes antiquing, or "junking" as she calls it. I go along with her when she asks me for I know her call means, "I am having a time with depression today; let's go out together." When you are the recipient of such a call, be flexible, drop your plans for the afternoon, forget the needlepoint you intended to finish, the curtains you were going to wash, practice "practical neglect" and "positive procrastination." In responding to your friend's need, you yourself will greatly benefit. It is important to learn to permit the "coulds" sometimes to replace the "shoulds" in your life.

Perhaps the depression has struck at a time when you cannot leave your house—in the middle of a heavy snow or rain storm, or when your car is not in service, or when you have a cold and know you have no business going out in inclement weather. Then, be your own psychiatrist. Try to analyze what exactly has set off your depression. A sad letter from a friend? Inability to cope with a difficult problem you are facing? Someone who owes you money and your unwillingness to ask him for it? An unpleasant letter you know you must write and keep putting off?

If there is some specific problem that you can rectify by taking care of the matter by phone, or letter, or a face-to-face talk, do it right away and relieve your mind of the nagging problem. If it is something you can do nothing about, acknowledge the fact, then turn the matter over to the Lord in prayer, "Casting all your cares upon him; for he careth for you" (I Peter 5:7).

If your spirit is still restless and disturbed, try the simple instructions my daughter gave her youngest when he was running restlessly through the house: "Sit down on the sofa, Jeremy, and say, 'Calm my spirit, Lord. Calm my spirit.' " As children of the Heavenly Father, there are times when you and I need to sit quietly before him and ask him to "Calm my spirit. Calm my spirit." It helps to try the psychological approach by repeating, "Thank You, Lord, for calming my spirit," over and over if necessary.

It is of great help to read the Psalms in times of distress. Find the ones that are especially suitable to your needs; the old standbys such as the 23rd, 94th, 100th, 139th can always be depended upon to bring healing to the soul.

Make a list of blessings and you will find the words of the old hymn "Count your blessings, name them one by one, and it will surprise you what the Lord has done. . ." are true and the heaviness of your depression will lighten.

The reading of poetry is very beneficial, if you read true poetry and not the ravings of some depressed, suicidal poet. I am including a poem I wrote in the midst of a depressed mood which completely lifted my spirit and made my blue day turn to sparkling green and gold:

> O, for the Joy-tossed Things of Spring—
> confetti on an apple bough
> a red bud's flame, tree-caught
> a thousand crocus heads yellow, purple
> rioting in winter beds
> jonquils hitch-hiking with golden thumbs
> alerting April on up-down hills
> pussy willows purring in the sun
> and lilacs making every bush
> they hold sway on a royal throne
> and small stones hand-thrown
> skipping on surface waters
> matching the skipping in heart
> and feet renewed by tossing things—
> clouds on strings, rice at May-June weddings
> and a salad bowl of willows wading
> barefoot in a creek; and all the greens
> of a brown-world yielding
> to the reckless lowland
> highland flaunting of Spring!

Psychologists are finding the writing and reading of poetry greatly benefits persons who are suffering from emotional illnesses. In Dr. Leedy's book, *The Therapy of Poetry,* he relates an account of a young woman who was desperately ill in a mental hospital with a condition caused by her inability to swallow any food. Someone brought her an anthology of poetry and, to the amazement of her doctors, within a short time her spirit and body relaxed, and she was cured of her throat paralysis. Poetry had worked on both her spirit and her body, and how closely the two are interrelated.

I have had numerous experiences with my own poetry where God has used it to minister, to uplift, and to comfort. One such instance involved a young woman who had tried to commit suicide. A mutual friend sent her my volume *I Need A Miracle Today, Lord*. Later she wrote me a heart-warming letter in which she thanked me for "transferring my faith to her"—she actually found strength in the words so that she could face the future.

Another specific example of the Lord's using a poem to lift the depression of a grieving person stems from the poem, "Planning."

A young man met a tragic death on his way home from a mission banquet when his car swerved head-on into a tree. Upon hearing of the tragedy, I wrote the following poem and sent it to his family.

> They said it was an accident
> that caused this new-turned grave.
> There blending gold with amber dawn,
> I see the wheat field wave.
> Last spring, the earth lay bare and brown
> beneath the turn of plow.
> Furrowed by plowman's guilding hand—
> ah see the wheat field now!
> Both furrows call for planning—field
> or grave. Grain, or soul,
> both know Master-planning.
> Sure Harvest is Your goal.

Later, I found that his father had been overcome with grief by his son's death. He sat in his chair staring vacantly into space, refusing to talk to anyone, or to eat. He was a farmer. An injury to his foot had made it impossible for him to work in his fields so his son, in addition to a night job, had been working days in the fields. Overfatigued, he had gone to sleep at the wheel and met his death. The father blamed himself and was completely immobilized by grief, depression, and apathy. Upon reading the poem, his wife told me later, the awful weight upon him was lifted, and he was able to go ahead with the funeral arrangements and other demands of living. The words of a simple poem reached him when even his pastor had not been able to get through to him!

There are numerous poets who have given to the world poetry that is uplifting and helpful, often written in their own severe trials and spiritual dilemmas. A poem need not be a happy one in order to ease depression. For example, how many times since Christina Rossetti wrote it has the following poem, although on a sad theme, eased the reader's grief?

> When I am dead, my dearest,
> Sing no sad songs for me;
> Plant thou no roses at my head
> Nor shady cypress tree.
>
> Be the green grass above me
> With shadows and dewdrops wet
> And if thou wilt, remember,
> And if thou wilt, forget.

I shall not see the shadows,
I shall not feel the rain,
I shall not hear the nightingale
Sing on, as if in pain;

And dreaming through the twilight
that doth not rise nor set,
Haply I may remember
And haply may forget.

Some years ago, the Clement Stone Foundation offered a $100 prize for an article on what had proved to be of greatest inspiration and help in the writer's life. The winner was a woman who wrote an article on a little volume of collected poetry that she had found a constant source of inspiration whenever she had needed it through the years. Poetry is second only to the Bible in its ability to lift the depressed spirit. Poetry is food for the soul.

During depression, the body, too, needs to be fed. When God spoke to Elijah as he sat downcast under the withered Juniper, he told him to "Arise and eat." It is no time to fast when you are suffering from depression. Eat your favorite food, be it a certain candy bar, or ice cream, or popcorn, or apples, or fried chicken. Treat yourself to your favorite "consolation" food. This advice is only for the times when you are actually suffering from depression. Don't make it a daily habit to console yourself by eating—unless you want to enter a circus sideshow billed as "the world's fattest woman!"

Depression and dieting do not mix. They are like oil and water. Nor does dieting mix with social dinners. Dieting is strictly a private matter and should not be inflicted on your hostess who may have spent hours in her kitchen preparing special foods and can be completely frustrated by the guest who unwisely says, "Oh, I am sorry but I am not eating any carbohydrates, just salads!" When you are away from home, eat with appreciation for your hostess' efforts. Keep your dieting for your own kitchen.

Spending an hour in a greenhouse or conservatory among green growing plants is an almost sure cure for depression—especially if you choose a plant for someone who is ill or going through a difficult life experience.

Working in a garden, feeling the live soil between your fingers, the sun warming your face, and hearing the birds singing in the trees and bushes around you, can lift the heavy burden and return the joy of living to your soul.

How long has it been since you walked in your city park? Take a small child with you—and don't forget to take along some bread to feed the pigeons on the sidewalks or the mallards on the lagoon.

For years, Chicago had its "Pigeon Annie" who could be seen any day in the week tossing crumbs from the huge bag she carried to the pigeons on the city streets. Old and alone in life, she had taken on a mission that must have given her much joy—and brought smiles to the faces of the people who saw her daily carrying out her purpose.

It is hard to maintain a depression in a zoo. The roaring of the lions, the antics of the monkeys, the barking of the seals can soon distract you from your world of gloom and make you realize that God, the Creator, has a sense of humor. It helps to remember this when a day closes in on you and tries to keep you in a strait jacket of self-pity.

In reality, if you will examine your depression closely,

you will find it strongly resembles the old scratchy wool underwear of self-pity. It is possible to let depression become a security blanket that, like the crawling infant, you drag from room to room, or house to house, wherever you go.

Depression is never God-given. Its roots are ugly and tangled in the mire of satanic defeat. It is an invisible quick-sand to trap and pull you in over your head, to suffocate you in its muck before you know it.

For years I suffered from migraine headaches that responded to no known medicine. Caffeine, often used to alleviate the pain of the migraine, was among my allergies and actually one of the causes of my headaches. One day I read a newspaper article on "biofeedback," a theory developed by the Menninger Institute. Upon the appearance of the first aura of the visual disturbance that normally precedes the true migraine, the Institute recommended that the patient lie down in a quiet room, close the eyes, clench the fists and slowly opening them repeating, "It is a beautiful world and I am so happy in it." Next, the migraine sufferer was to imagine that the hands were extremely warm, burning over a fire or under a hot sun, or wearing woolen mittens. With practice, the temperature in the hands actually is elevated by blood being drawn from the head (where the arteries have become swollen and the cause of the pain) and the headache is relieved. Since learning the simple exercise, I have been entirely free from the migraines that plagued me for years.

It occurred to me that if biofeedback could control migraines, it could also help route depression. I recommend lying down, flat on your back, close your eyes, clenching your fists over your breast and slowly open them as you move your hands to your sides while repeating, "You have made a beautiful world, God, and I am happy in it." I cannot guarantee that it will work for you, but it will help you to realize that you are still a part of God's beautiful world and your inherent right is the joy of living.

As you lie in your room, imagine yourself walking along a beach, watching the sun play on the waves. Now go for a mental stroll in a deep woods or in a lovely garden. Recall the most beautiful place in your memory. For me, this is a lake at sunset in Loveland, Colorado, where we spent a vacation. Place yourself in this beautiful place in your memory and thank God for everything you possibly can—for the difficult things as well as for the good. "And we know that all things work together for good to them that love God, to them who are called according to his purpose" (Romans 8:28).

Depression is not for the Christian. You anticipate the Joy of the Resurrection and know that every hour you live draws you closer to that glorious hour when you shall see the Creator of us all who will have with Him those we love and have lost for only a little while.

> Teach me to sing a psalm, Lord
> on the sidewalk of every day
> not to reserve my song for choir,
> country retreat meadowed
> with larks on fences.
>   This sidewalk has no larks
>   to sing—mine must be
>   the birdsong here
>   above the litter
>   of last night's paper plates,

cola cans and debris
that gutter the morning.
Here, Lord, where a song
is needed—I would sing
a sidewalk psalm
sun-flecked with sparrow chirp,
Creator-God, to Thee.

9

Living Your Own Life

If there is one word to describe the eminent difference between the married woman and the woman who lives alone it is "resourcefulness."

I have just come from a luncheon where one of the women told about finding a chameleon in her mobile home. "What did you do about it?" I asked.

"Oh, I just went next door for Bart to come and catch it for me," she exclaimed, "I just can't stand those things."

I laughed inwardly for I knew she was doing exactly what I would have done three years ago before my husband's debilitating illness.

Upon occasion before I had my chimney top screened, starlings would sometimes fall down into the fireplace. This was always the cause of a lot of excitement and usually I would secure the fireplace screen with some heavy object and wait for my husband or son to come home and remove the frightened birds.

One evening recently I returned home to hear a strange, but familiar noise coming from the fireplace.

Sure enough, there were two starlings trapped in the ashes. My immediate reaction was to scream for someone to help. But there was no one within screaming distance. Should I phone my son in the next town, bother my good neighbor, or call the police? I decided it was time to grow up and take care of the problem myself. I pulled the drapes over the windows, opened the front door, and arming myself with a broom, I removed the fireplace screen and let the two startled black birds hobble into the living room. Calmly on the outside, but with much trepidation on the inside, I got behind them and witch-like shooed them before my broom, away from the piano, the paintings on the wall, into the entrance hall. For a moment my efforts almost met with failure for I had forgotten to cover the hall mirror, and both birds plunged dejectedly into the glass, but at last they found the front door and freedom.

Their freedom was no more real than mine in that I had conquered an area of weakness by solving my own problem. I could not have done this before my husband's illness. I went further than the immediate problem. When I had the house re-roofed, I arranged with the roofer to replace some bricks in the chimney along with a screen so birds could no longer fall down the long dark tunnel to the fireplace below.

Later, when I told my son about the birds I had shooed from the house, he stared at me for one long minute before saying, "Well, you are something!" And I felt a warm glow inside at my new and growing resourcefulness.

Some women are born with more resourcefulness than others, but everyone can cultivate the attribute, and there is nothing like living alone to encourage the cultivation.

In Mexico I was astonished to see so many women wearing drab black. Were they all widows? No, in Mexico a woman adopts widow's weeds when any member of her family dies, not just her husband. It is a form of mourning that she observes for the rest of her life. How very unfortunate. Colors can actually affect the way we feel. I find it unwise for me to wear black since my husband's illness unless I want to find myself feeling depressed.

We are fortunate in America that the year of wearing black is no longer expected, nor adhered to in most sections of the country. At a recent funeral, I was impressed to see the widow wearing a bright red coat. She was a fastidious woman of excellent taste who had loved her husband deeply for 57 years and this was like waving, or rather wearing, a victory flag that said, "I know Bill is alive and that I shall see him again even though his body is in this casket." She won the admiration of the mourners and also helped to set the triumphant tone of the whole service. What a contrast to the outcast widows of India and Iran and other pagan countries whose bodies in past centuries often were burned on their husbands' funeral pyres. Or, if they were permitted to live, they were herded like cattle into sections of the countryside or city where they died from neglect and starvation.

It is not easy to get used to the idea of not being "first place" in someone's life. You lived in the warmth of this cocoon for many years, and now the cocoon is gone and there is no one to shelter you from life's buffeting. No one to hear you scream and rescue you from a kitchen chair when a mouse frightens you! No one to back the car out of the garage on an icy day to keep you from sliding into something. No one to raise the stuck window. No one to discuss problems with and to help you make decisions.

You may never be "first place" in anyone's life again in this world. But remember, you have known love when there are many women who never have.

No matter how important your children, grandchildren, and friends are to you, they can never fill this "first place" position that your husband and you shared together. Realizing and facing up to a problem is the first step in solving it.

You are the crysallis emerging from the cocoon of your past life. You can either decide to fold your wings tightly to your inactive body and shrivel into a life of inactivity—or you can learn to use the wings you now have and experience solo flying into a vast and exciting world.

Do not waste your energy trying to solve the "why" of your loss. Perhaps you shall never know why.

Now is the time to deal with the what and how of your situation. Ask yourself, What shall I do about it? Or, how can I best live with the situation?

If you have ever watched a crysallis emerge from its cocoon, you will know that it does not burst forth and immediately soar into flight. It comes out slowly, tries out its wings by fluttering them slowly up and down — and then when they are strong enough and accustomed to the new life around them, the flight is attempted. First to a low bush, then to the low branch of a tree, and finally the blue sky and its freedom.

Try out your new wings gradually. For example, if

your husband has always done the driving on long trips, and your driving has been reserved for around town, do not plan a long cross country trip until you have gained confidence in your ability to drive for long distances. Try the shorter trips first, and ask a friend to go with you should you want to go on a longer journey.

Avoid quick, rash decisions. Caution is the word. Think the situation over carefully. Discuss it with close friends and family. Do not ask for straight advice for then you risk the chance of offending someone when you go against the advice she has offered. Say rather, "I would like to know what your opinion is on such and such. . ." The person will realize that you are considering perhaps several opinions and will not feel offended at your final decision. You are asserting your right to make up your own mind and follow out your own decision.

It is always amazing to me how other people (and well-meaning people) can so often know God's will for your life when you frankly have a hard time finding it for yourself—and what is even stranger, they admittedly have difficulty knowing God's will for their own direction.

I like the advice Dwight L. Moody gave a young man who wrote him asking how he could best serve the Lord. Moody's reply was "Serve him right where he has placed you—in your own town among the people you know." Travelling distances does not make the missionary, nor does crossing an ocean. Service to God is a matter of being, rather than going.

One well-adjusted friend who lost her husband five years ago sold her large home to her daughter and purchased a beautiful mobile home in a court close to her old home. In the winter months she pulls a 23-foot travel

trailer and spends much of her time near a Bible conference grounds where she has made many friends and has
found opportunity to be of service numerous times.
Frankly, she is more of a woman than I am for I cannot
quite see myself pulling a trailer cross country alone at
this point. Cross country travel in a car with the problems involved in keeping it travel-worthy are almost
more than the average woman can manage. Oh, for the
fortitude of our pioneer grandmothers who crossed
mountains and prairies on rutted wagon trails into the
vast unknown!

In our family tree is a great-great grandmother who met
Sherman's men at her plantation door, defiantly shook
the deed to her home in their faces and burned it in the
fireplace before their astonished eyes. She packed the
iron skillets, bedding and clothing into a wagon and fled
from Virginia into Texas where she knew her husband
was with the Confederate forces. No road maps, no way
stations, no grocery stores. . .only the will to find her
way to her destination. I am the owner of one of her iron
skillets and I never look at it without praying for some of
her courage and fortitude.

God has promised wisdom to all who ask and one of
the ways in which the woman alone will need special
insight is in determining what should be the emotional
center of her life. There is always the temptation to transfer her complete center of attention and affection to her
children—and often to expect the same attention in return. This is a disastrous course of action. You cannot
live vicariously in your children. True, you may feel your
children are extensions of your desires and your ambi-
tions and you may see some of your dreams fulfilled in
their lives. But there the fusion must cease—and it can-

not unless you determine to live your own life, to seek out avenues that interest you, occupations that are your cup of tea—and yours alone. When you develop interests of your own, you will find satisfaction in them, and not feel the need of living your children's lives.

Writers testify that the keeping of a daily record book is extremely valuable. You may never have considered doing this, but such a record can give the woman alone great help in clarifying her thinking and her direction. Write down your feelings, your ideas, your goals, your prayers. If you have never had time to keep a record in the past, you have now. That is one of the advantages of living alone. You are free to manage your time in the way you want to. Unfortunately, some women fall into the TV soap opera trap and waste valuable hours. I try to limit TV viewing to special programs that help to keep one informed; to the news and to the best of TV viewing—usually in the evening when I am too tired for more productive pursuits. Never let TV control your life.

During the first months of my living alone, I found that keeping the radio or TV on helped to make the house seem less lonely, but now I enjoy the quiet which affords time to write, to read and whatever.

What are you going to write in your journal? You are not a writer—you do not need to be to record your inmost thoughts, or events of historical value, or even the weather. Some of the pages in my journal are devoted to prayer requests and it is a joy to look back through these pages and to check off the answered prayers with praise to our wonderful Lord for His faithfulness. They are often a reminder of what worries I had all for nothing!

The widow who has developed a love for reading is most fortunate for "living in other men's minds." This is not only a way of escape when one's own world has turned gray and flat, but it is a way to extend the dimensions of your mind so that you are more able to cope with the problems you face. Spend time in your local library, browse through its shelves, keep abreast of the new books that are displayed in a prominent place. Read the magazines and listen to the new records in the record room. I never visit our library without coming away feeling refreshed and uplifted. Keep your library card active and use it to carry home books that interest you and deserve time spent in their pages.

Do not let yourself become a martyr to your widowhood. Oddly enough some women seem to enjoy their grief. They wear it around their shoulders like a costly mink stole. They serve it like caviar at their tables when they are alone or when they have guests. Look cooly at grief for what it is: a phase of life that everyone has to experience at some time or another. But it should never be allowed to become the dominating factor in life. Put on your red coat like my friend Ella and wear it triumphantly!

For many weeks after my husband was stricken, I could not go near a dress shop. I had utterly no interest in clothes at all. Finally, my family told me they were tired of seeing me in the same old clothes and would I please purchase something new. I found the dark colors appealed to me, but I knew they would do nothing for my mood and spirit. I purchased a persimmon colored pant suit and was amazed what it did for my returning moral.

In his famous play, *A Doll's House*, Ibsen's Nora complains to Torwald in the first (and last) conversation they have as equals:

You have always been kind to me, But our home has been nothing but a playroom. I have been your doll-wife, just as at home I was papa's doll-child; and here the children have been my dolls. I thought it great fun when you played with me, just as you thought it great fun when I played with them. That is what our marriage has been, Torwald.

And when her husband reminded her that before all else she was a wife and mother:

"I don't believe that any longer," she replied. "I believe that before all else I am a reasonable human being, just as you are—or—at all events—that I must try to become one."

Your days of "playing house," if that is the way it was with you, are over. Now it is time to grow up into a mature woman thrilled with the challenge of all life holds out to you.

Who knows, you may be standing on the verge of a new and exciting career. Keep your mind open to any and all possibilities. Never let yourself think that for you life is over. It most assuredly is not — unless you permit it to be. "Grow old along with me," wrote Browning, "the best is yet to be!" Although the one person you wanted to grow old with is out of your life, there are some wonderful relationships and experiences ahead of you.

When life seems to be a series of meaningless days and aimless nondirection, then may be the time to take on a new project. Paper a bedroom which may have been needing it for years. "Me paper a room?" "Me" may be surprised at what me can do! Look through the wallpaper books, choose a pattern that does not need to be matched and you are on your way. If you use the pre-pasted, it is easy to do a few strips at a time, and before you know it you will be pleased with the freshness of your room. If you are afraid to tackle it alone the first time, ask a friend to help you, and in turn, volunteer your help in one of her projects. A wallpapering party can be fun—provided not too many persons try to crowd into a room at the same time.

An elderly woman told me one time when I exclaimed over how beautifully she kept her home, "I just do a little bit at a time—one window, one cupboard, one floor. That way I never have to clean house and get my whole house upset." Her house was always clean and she was never worn out from the customary "spring housecleaning."

This is good psychology towards accomplishing any task. A little bit at a time, and you may see your small Rome built. Have you been wanting to write a book? Fifteen minutes a day and at the end of a year, you, if you keep at it faithfully, will find you have your manuscript, at least your first draft, completed.

Has playing the piano, or guitar, been your secret unfulfilled desire? One-half hour a day can make you realize fulfillment as the months go by.

Or is it painting? Purchase an instruction book and an easel. Acrylics are much simpler for the amateur than oils. Invite a friend in to "splash" with you, or sign up for an art class—and you may find that your state has its own Grandma Moses.

Many of the handcraft shops are delightful places to

learn macramé, knitting, crochet, or the popular decoup-age. Do you find it hard to go alone to such a place? Then invite a friend who may be having a hard time going places alone also.

A friend of mine returned to college when her husband died—at the age of 59—and obtained her degree at 63. She had to push a little bit on the door to the classrooms, but a new world opened up to her. Although she had spent years of her married life working as a bookkeeper, since completing her education, she has written three successful books.

If you find going to the old places where you and your husband went together difficult, choose to go places where he did not go with you. This may mean a new church, and a new club, and vacation spots where you did not go together. "His mercies are new every morning," writes the psalmist. He knows your needs and wants to meet them.

In Francis A. Schaeffer's book, *How Should We Then Live?*, he writes that Jean-Jacques Rousseau (1712-1778), the philosopher, ran into problems with the humanism of the High Renaissance and found that when God and man, his created being, were presumed to be a part of the cosmic world, both became lost to society. God and man are separate entities from the cosmic world. True at times man is subject to it as when he rushes out in front of a car, or into the path of a hurricane, but his thoughts are capable of transcending the cosmic world about him and communicating with God. Such a feeling of being completely a part of and subject to the cosmic world can leave the widow devastated (and even Rousseau commit-ted suicide) but the fact that God is in control of the

cosmic world, and she can communicate with him, the
Giver of every Good Gift and of Life itself, is a tremen-
dously motivating factor in her life.

I CANNOT SAY THAT I AM "NOTHING," LORD

> when You made me.
> I am your handwork,
> made in Your image,
> a triune being: body,
> soul and spirit. O, I have slid
> below Your Standards,
> far below, and I have cost
> You Calvary, but I know
> Your redeeming love.
> > Would You have died
> > for "nothing," Lord?
> > No,
> > I am the person You bought.

10

Without Whose Absence

A writer once dedicated his book to his wife with the following words: "To my dear wife, without whose absence this book could not have been written."

Time is the new commodity your widowhood has brought you. Time that may be used as you desire. Time of which you have the power to prove to be either a good steward or a poor one. Now you may ask yourself "What is it that I always wanted to do when my husband was living that I could not do because he did not like the activity, the game, the company, or whatever?"

Some women who have been married to men who did not like to travel find that their widowhood has provided them with both the money and the freedom to travel—when and where they choose. This freedom to travel is to be listed among the assets of being a widow—and we need to count *all* the assets we can find.

The mother of one of my friends has travelled around the world since her doctor husband's death—not on expensive luxury liners but on smaller passenger lists on freighters. While freighter travel is diminishing in availability, it is still possible for bookings at certain seasons of the year for travel to Europe, Asia, South America, Africa, and to many islands of the sea. The accommodations are quite pleasant and passengers enjoy more free time with less social pressures than the often overly planned activities of the luxury, city-on-rudder, type of travel. Your travel agency can supply you with information about freighter travel availability.

The choice of a good travel agent can prove to be highly beneficial. My travel agent is an older woman who runs her own travel agency, a small two-woman operation, but I feel she gives me exceptional service and advice.

If travelling is your thing, a little planning and forethought can not only save you money, but often provide you with better accommodations. Travel scheduled a little off season, such as Florida in April or May, October or November, rather than in the peak of the winter months, offers hotel accommodations for half the rate they charge at the season's height—as well as avoiding the pushing, shoving crowds of people. There are also excursion rates, week-end, and night coach fares that cut the cost of air travel, but you will need to get your reservations in early.

You will need to inquire yourself about such savings as too often travel agents will not advise you of them, because they realize a greater percentage on your higher travel costs. I recently called an airline to change from day coach to a night reservation and was informed "____ Airline does not have a night flight going to Chicago." By asking if there was a night flight on another airline, I was able to save $20.

In my mail today came a letter from the president of a

Christian college inviting me to join a summer tour to Reformation country in a three-week excursion to Europe that he and his wife are leading. I know the couple well and know that anyone fortunate enough to sign up for their tour would have a most enjoyable and informative summer.

Travelling with a tour group is a fine way to see various countries in the company of usually congenial people and an opportunity to form enduring friendships. It is often preferable to find an interested friend to go along with you. That way you know you will have a congenial roommate.

Travelling with a tour group, led by reputable leaders, guarantees activities in which you may be delighted to participate. If night club life holds no interest for you, tours that make a point of visiting such attractions may be avoided by carefully selecting tours that are more interested in the aesthetic and cultural advantages. The tour leader is most often responsible for the type of activity that will be involved. Some mission groups hold annual tours to their specific mission fields. This is a good way to combine missionary interest and sight seeing.

Another positive result from the loss of your mate is the power to choose where you will live. In town, or in the country? In the northwoods, or in the sunny southland? Or, perhaps both? The latter choice must be seriously thought out for it is easy to become "building poor" and to find yourself encumbered by too many buildings on which you must pay the costs of both maintenance and taxes.

Your housing needs have changed overnight. Perhaps you are still living in the large family home in which you and your husband reared your brood. But where are you going to move? Also, you need to answer the question, "Am I emotionally stable enough to stand the additional stress of moving?"

Among my acquaintances, I have observed that some widows are seemingly happier to have remained in their family homes than some who have sold and moved into hotels or apartments. Living with happy memories can prove an asset to some women in the adjustment to widowhood. They can still hear the hum of the electric razor coming from the bathroom in the morning, footsteps returning on the walk in the evening.

Again, an apartment may be the answer for you. It offers the advantage of no grass to mow in summer and no walks to shovel in winter. It means that there are close-by neighbors and someone else to care for the plumbing.

You may be among those women who are not at all apartment oriented. You may prefer a town house or a condominium. Many articles have been written for and against the condominium. Among the pros are the availability of a club house, tennis courts, swimming pools, and a certain comaraderie with other condominium owners. On the con side, maintenance costs are subject to the vote of the condominium owners—and you may find yourself paying more for maintenance than you did in your house. At present, the economy in Florida as well as in Illinois and other parts of the country has been glutted with condominiums and they are very slow in finding buyers. This makes a buyer's market and is an advantage should you decide to buy now, but it could well prove to be a disadvantage if you want to sell in the near future. However, this situation is expected to change and even reverse itself in the near future.

Real estate is still considered to be the best investment there is in this inflationary market. This may make it advisable if you sell your home to reinvest in another piece of real estate in order to take advantage of this investor's market.

Where I live there are many widows (26 in number) living alone in their mobile homes. This gives a strong feeling of community with a very economical mode of living. There are common laundry facilities and a common well for water which is piped to each lot and is included in the low monthly maintenance cost. There is an obvious pride in ownership and the small yards and patios boast many varieties of tropical shrubs, palms and flowers. The mutually owned club house is a center for social activities, and vespers on Sunday evening.

Nearby shopping centers and churches are additional bonuses to living in the court. I am grateful to the Lord for this place and for the feeling of security that results from being encircled by close neighbors who note any strangers coming in and out of the court's one entrance.

When we reach the time we no longer need our large houses, nor have the energy to care for the yards surrounding them, then it is time to consider the apartment, the town house, the condominium, the smaller home, the mobile home, and the retirement center. Many find they can be very happy in the more simplified way of living which the mobile home or retirement center provides. Here in Florida, heating costs are all but non-existent, the water is provided with the maintenance cost, and electricity is a necessity wherever one chooses to live. Of course, air conditioning in summer adds to the electric bill more than it does when living further north.

There are two types of mobile courts: one that is

owned by a private person or corporation, an investment group, or sometimes a town, in which rents are levied on the lots although the trailer is owned by the buyer. Such rental is subject to continual raises (sometimes unfair and unwarranted). Some rentals in Florida have gone from $25 a month to $250 in a space of three years. Owning a trailer on such precarious rental property can prove hazardous also for when the rent soars too high, many owners put their trailers up for sale in an effort to avoid the high rental costs and this floods the market, making trailer sales in such a court difficult. Sometimes there are poorly enforced regulations which result in undisciplined children, barking dogs, blaring TVs and noisy parties at night, all of which can prove most disconcerting when you have reached a time in life when you appreciate quiet.

In the first type of mobile court, the trailer owner has little or nothing to say about the rent costs, the making and enforcing of court rules, or the selection of would-be renters.

In the second type of mobile court such as we bought into in Monet Acres, the court is owned by the members of the community, and you as a lot purchaser become a member and have a vote in the business sessions, a say in the maintenance costs levied and in the purchase of new equipment, etc. The trailer owner is free to sell his trailer and move it off the lot and to replace it with a different trailer at any time he desires. Buyers into the park must go through a screening committee. They cannot be over 68 years of age, and if they desire to have small children living with them for any length of time they must obtain the permission of the board of trustees. This is to prevent undisciplined children from becoming rowdy and annoying the residents. Animals are not allowed.

This type of mobile court is owned by a corporation formed by the buyers. It is modeled after the condominium apartment, or rather it would be more correct to say the condominium apartment is modeled after the court in Monet Acres. Monet Acres was the first court to incorporate and set up regulations which have been used as guidelines by condominiums not only in Florida but in other parts of the country as well. Expenses are kept to a minimum in Monet where majority rule is monitored by the retirees who are interested in the economy of living.

There are also apartment buildings for retirees which are not available to anyone under 60. These are often quite advantageous for the widow who qualifies.

The retirement center often requires a good sized initial investment plus a monthly rental fee and many times the investment is absorbed by the center and lost to your estate's heirs. It has the disadvantage of being difficult to move from in case you are dissatisfied with living conditions. The advantages are that there are also built-in provisions such as meals available, common dining rooms, entertainment centers, and often a nursing center in case of illness.

The power of choice carries with it the need for discretion. You no longer have your husband to guard your spending. (And rare is the man who didn't do this!) "Shall I purchase a new refrigerator this year? Or carpeting?" No one says, "No, I don't think we can afford it." There is money in the bank so why not, you ask yourself. Here you must remind yourself that you are the sole monitor of your money, the comptroller of your checking account. And if your husband was shrewd and careful in his spending, you may ask yourself the question he might have asked were he living, "Do you really need new carpeting?" You may find it wise to keep your old refrigerator as long as it is in good working condition and to forego the carpeting until you decide whether or not you will stay or move from your present residence.

You must guard your spending for there are always unforeseen expenses that may come. A new water heater. A new roof. New gutters. Or new eye glasses. Or expensive dental work. There is no one to share these unexpected expenses now. Perhaps the rule is: "avoid the unnecessary expenses so as to have money for the necessary expenses that arise."

No change should be made in a hurry. Nor under the pressure of well-meaning family and friends. There are many factors to be considered in moving from your present residence—and at the head of the list is location. In real estate there is the time-worn story about the real estate man who taught his underlings, "What are the three most important factors in purchasing real estate?" And the answer was, "one—location; two—location; and three—location."

The little home in the country may be inviting, but it is seldom for the widow. The home in Arizona may also seem to be what you have always wanted—but this too may be a poor choice if it means settling in a community where you know no one, or have few friends and no family, and cannot get on a doctor's patient list. You are now approaching a time in life when family, friends and doctors are all important in your life and may become increasingly more so as the years go by.

One friend considered buying a house at the top of a steep hill—difficult to reach on foot in summer and by car in the winter. The house was quaint but it belonged to her youth and did not fit into her middle-aged plans. She settled for a house near the business section in the small town in which she lived. This way she could walk to the super market, the library, the drug store without having to drive a car, or depending upon someone else to serve as taxi.

Another friend gave up her large home to live with an unmarried daughter in a summer resort town. But a serious heart attack caused her to move to an apartment near a hospital in order to be close to medical care when it was needed. Being close to good medical care is vitally important and a factor to be considered in making a change, especially if you suffer from heart trouble or other chronic diseases.

Another plus under the power of choice available to a widow is the selection of food. You have no one else's food likes and dislikes to consider when you go to the super market. You may purchase what you like. Here, too, wisdom is needed. While it may be advisable in deep depression to let food compensate, it is unfortunate to develop a habit of using food likes and dislikes for compensation for unhappiness, self-pity, and remorse. Consolation foods are usually full of calories and before you know it, you may find you have gained five or ten pounds—or more! Diet is important in order to maintain good health and the proper weight.

This is a good time to read and reread good diet books and articles on health. Some are far-out, but others if adhered to can definitely improve health and alter weight problems. Much is being written about the DNA and RNA factors since the discovery of the Double Helix. High on the list in the DNA foods are anchovies, kidneys, liver, meat extracts, sardines, sweetbreads. Listed as next in value are: fish, dried beans, dried lentils, dried peas, shellfish; and in the medium category are: caviar, bran, asparagus, brains, beets, fish roe, oatmeal, mushrooms, onions, spinach, nuts, radishes, wheat germ, poultry. Among the low foods having the DNA factor are: breads, cheese, cereals, gelatin, fruits, butter, fats, eggs, milk, most vegatables, sugar, sweets. DNA is the factor that is supposed to keep one young and retard aging.

While volumes are being written about dieting for good health, basically the experts agree on the following: the elimination of sweets, pastries, confections and artificial foods; stressing fresh fruits, vegetables, whole grain cereal; emphasizing protein rather than carbohydrates, especially in fish, poultry and lean meats.

It is in your power to choose to be well and healthy. It is money-saving and far more pleasant than being ill. Good health is doubly important for you now since there is no one to bring you a cup of hot tea, or an aspirin should you come down with influenza or a more serious illness.

As you know, exercise too is important. Walking is the cheapest form of exercise and the most accessible. It requires no experience or training, no expensive equipment—only good walking shoes. You can do it alone without waiting for someone to walk with you. Walk on short errands where you are tempted to drive your car. It saves gasoline as well as improving both your health and the appearance of your figure.

There may be a form of exercise you enjoyed in the past but your husband didn't, so you gave it up. Swimming is in this category for me and last summer I joined my nieces in swimming in a near-by pool and was pleased

I could still do the strokes I had learned as a child. I admit the figure I now display is far from what it was 30 years ago—but maybe, just maybe, it will improve along with my breast stroke and surface dives.

I love to walk in summer, but in the cold weather I can no longer stand the brisk, biting air. I have solved this, however, by walking in the enclosed shopping malls when the weather is inclement. There is some risk here, however, and that is of allowing the window-shopping to prove too inviting and become reality-shopping.

In my trailer court is a lovely woman who has kept her husband from a wheel chair by what she terms "pattern dancing." Twenty years ago her husband had plastic sockets inserted in both hips and the doctors thought he would never walk again. But wise Signe taught him "pattern dancing" and today he is far from a wheel chair victim. Numbers of other residents who were bothered with arthritis came to the classes and have benefitted. Folk dancing is a good form of exercise if you are not inhibited by strict fundamental teachings.

Tennis and golf are also excellent forms of exercise as is the newer sport of racquetball. Table tennis may be preferable for persons with circulatory problems to any of these more strenuous sports. Tennis courts are available in public parks and handball courts are in most YMCAs or YWCAs. These organizations have fine health programs and a membership can provide assets for both physical and fellowship needs. The purchase of a bicycle may prove a good investment in both health and gasoline savings.

As a widow your power of choice extends to many areas. You may choose your time of going to bed or rising in the morning. If you are a morning person and you were married to a night owl, this may be a special plus for you.

Or perhaps you loved house plants and your husband objected to living in a jungle. You are free to clutter your house with as many as your heart desires. They do require attention and watering. They can add a type of presence that lessens the loneliness you may be feeling. However, the most important Presence of all is the Holy Spirit who can be your constant companion, removing all feeling of loneliness, and guiding you in making the right choices now that you are alone.

"For I am persuaded, that neither death, nor life, nor angels, nor principalities, nor powers, nor things present, nor things to come, nor height, nor depth, nor any other creature, shall be able to separate us from the love of God, which is in Christ Jesus our Lord"—(Romans 8:38, 39).

11

On Becoming
Too Involved in
Your Children's Lives

In Joe Bayly's Sunday School class, I recently heard him make the statement, "One of the greatest problems in America today is that parents let their children become the center of the home, then when the children are gone, the marriage falls apart. Children are a transitory experience—here today, and gone tomorrow."

It is easy for a married couple to be so overjoyed by the birth of a child that they permit that child to become the hub around which they, the spokes, revolve. When a parent dies, it becomes easy for the parent left to make the child or children of the marriage the center of interest.

But this is not what God intended. He wants to be the Hub. When the children are given the hub position, where God rightfully belongs, the wheel is off balance and it cannot function smoothly. This is true whether one or both parents are living. Along with the parents, children are spokes in the family and God must be given the center position.

It is quite a natural thing for a widow to turn to her

children for comfort, for support, for companionship to replace the immense gap in her life. For a short time such a relationship may be desirable and can be of mutual benefit in adjusting to the loss of a loved father and husband.

But there comes a time when the continued instrinsic relationship can prove detrimental both to the children and to the widow. Almost before she realizes what is happening, the widow may find herself wrapped entirely in her children's lives with no interests and social life of her own. This is very sad when it happens and too often it is the case when a family is closely knit.

Women who allow themselves to sink into the trap of living on the fringe of their children's lives are for the most part an unhappy lot. Frictions often develop between the children and their parents: "Must we take your mother with us on our vacation? Can't we have just one vacation without her?" "Does she have to come to dinner at the same time my parents are going to be here?" These and many similar questions become all too common in the home where mother has become the several-times-a-week guest and always-on-Sundays-and-holidays.

Oh, her son-in-law is a wonderful fellow and never in the world would he say anything to hurt her or do anything really to keep her out of their lives.

Then, there are the grandchildren and the constant demands in the way of baby sitting which as a grandmother she can easily fill—and without pay. She wouldn't think of taking any money for baby sitting her grandchildren, even though in some instances she could well use the money.

But after all, she may not really know what is going on

in her wonderful son-in-law's mind. She might be greatly surprised and hurt if she could read his thoughts. It is only normal for a man to like to have the complete attention of his wife and children. He married the daughter so that he could be with her day in and day out. You, dear grandmother, although you may be sweet and charming and everyone loves you, are an outsider in your daughter's home. Don't ever let yourself forget this fact—and it will spare both you and your children a lot of unnecessary heartache.

Louise Mathew, a lovely Christian woman, was resented by her daughter and her husband because she insisted on continuing to do many things for and lavishing all kinds of gifts on her daughter after she was married. It was frustrating for the son-in-law to have her beat him to fulfilling a need or desire, and where she could have been deeply loved had she exercised discretion, she was only tolerated. Finally, upset by her mother constantly bursting in on the family's privacy, the daughter suggested that she not come unless she were asked. Of course, the overly zealous mother was deeply offended. Imagine having to be invited to her own daughter's home! But it was the only protection the daughter had against her invasion of privacy.

"Where you are much wanted, go little, where you are little wanted, go not at all." The old adage has much wisdom in it and is a good rule for the new widow to remember where her married children are concerned.

It is a good feeling to have them phone and say, "Where on earth have you been? We have been trying to reach you for three days!" Or, "Why don't you ever come over? We haven't seen you for ages and the children are begging to see you!"

I have the peculiar situation of having my two daughters married to ministers and my son who is in seminary serving as an assistant pastor in a church. There are three churches involved and I am constantly asked, "Why don't you put your membership in my church?" I visit their respective churches and am vitally interested in their ministries, but I do not feel that this gives me license to become a member of any of the three churches. I admit it has been hard for me to go back to the church, or I should say churches, my husband and I attended together. I have recently been visiting other churches, one in particular where I know some of the women in the women's work, and am praying about placing my membership there. I must not only have a life of my own but a church life of my own as well.

Can you see the situation? I go to my son's morning service. After the service although he was planning to ask another couple home for dinner, he and his wife invite me instead. Not knowing about the other couple, I accept the invitation. The next Sunday after church I say, "Why not let me take you and Mary out to dinner—Mary has worked hard all week and needs a treat."

If I were to do this Sunday after Sunday, it would soon interfere with their social life and even their ministry in their church. This I must not allow to happen.

About grandchildren. Your daughter or son does not have the same ideas about rearing children as you had about rearing yours. For example, you never permitted snacking before a meal. Your six-year-old grandchild (who is the delight of your life) comes in before supper and helps himself to a piece of bread with peanut butter and jelly. You immediately take it away from him and say,

"Oh Jeremy, you must not eat before your supper." Grandson number two asks, surprised, "Why not? Mommy always lets us!" Immediately you are in hot water for no matter how much better your house rules were to your way of thinking, this is your daughter's home, her children, and her house rules. You have no right to—that important word again—"interfere" or perhaps more accurately "meddle." If this incident happens when you are merely visiting, think how many things there would be in which you and your daughter would disagree were you to actually move into her home.

You believed in strict discipline. Beds were made before leaving the room. Pajamas hung up. Books were kept on the book shelves. "A place for everything and everything in its place." Your mother taught you the phrase, and you have lived by it. Your daughter may be a much more permissive mother, yet in no way a less desirable or effective one. Little things like clothing not hung up immediately and beds not made do not annoy her at all. She does insist on very polite table manners, however, and you find yourself wanting to ask, "Why do you insist on Jeremy folding his napkin so precisely and waiting until he has permission before he leaves the table? It does not seem at all consistent to me with the snacking before meals you permit." It does not have to be consistent. This is your daughter's home and she makes the rules—not you—no matter how much older and wiser you may think you are.

Never interfere with your children disciplining your grandchildren. They have the right to set up disciplinary measures according to what they believe to be right and effective. Your days for disciplining are over. Enjoy the grandchildren. Don't be a bossy old grandmother that no one likes. It is more important to be loved by your grand-child than to be the one who makes him mind. They expect and accept discipline from their parents, but they may only resent it from you. Children should not have to answer to too many bosses, and you come in the "too many" category.

Of course, there are extreme cases such as a daughter's illness where she may be too ill to take charge and care for her children and where you may have to step in and substitute for her—but be sure whatever discipline you may have to exercise is discipline that is in line with her teachings.

It is not easy to be a wise parent, and it is even more difficult to be a wise mother-in-law. But it is far easier to maintain a good relationship when you go only occasionally to your children's homes, and much more difficult when you go more often, and all but impossible when you live with your children.

Moving in with one's children does not solve the widow's problems; it may quite frankly multiply them. There is no house that is large enough for two families to dwell together harmoniously, especially when there are two or three generations represented.

We are sometimes reminded of the good old days when the grandparents lived with the second and third generation, and everyone got along just fine. But this description has been glossed over by the years and if the truth were known, there were back then some very difficult problems in the three-generation household. We may not hear about them, but they existed.

It is difficult for a mother and daughter or daughter-in-law to manage a kitchen jointly. No two women have the same ideas about how a kitchen should be run. Often the mother will take over despite her determination not to do so. Soon the daughter becomes dependent upon the mother for decisions of what to buy at the store, and what to plan for meals. No matter how gracious the son-in-law may appear on the surface, he can never be entirely happy with such an arrangement. He prefers to have his wife reigning in her own kitchen, and he can only feel resentment for anything or anyone who prevents her being queen of her home.

When we retired in a cold climate, we were strongly tempted by the urging of our daughter and son-in-law in Florida to purchase a home in the warm clime and move to the area in which they live. Although he liked the town in which they lived, my husband, being a wise man, thought it unwise to buy there, but preferred a mobile home 30 miles away. This distance permitted both families to have separate lives. Since his illness, I have toyed with the idea of moving permanently to the town in which they live, but I know his reasoning was wise and therefore have decided against such a move.

Often a parent will move to a town where a child has settled and within a year or so, the son or son-in-law will be transferred or have a better job opportunity offered him in another city. The parent will have to decide whether to go or stay, and as one's age increases, it becomes more difficult to move. Young people are more capable of adapting to new circumstances and flying with the frisbee. Making new friends is not as easy in the 50s or 60s as it was in the 20s.

Sometimes a son will refuse a better position because he does not want to move away from the parent who has followed his move once already. This is not fair to him or to his family. The fact that our daughter lived in a nearby town was a factor in the purchase of our mobile home, but we asked ourselves, "Would we make this purchase if our daughter did not live where she did?" The answer was yes.

May Parrish has had her mother-in-law in her home for 30 years. Mother Parrish was a very demanding woman and although she had her own living room and bedroom, her life centered in the living room, dining room and kitchen of the family. The Parrishes were fine Christian people who set high standards for their five daughters. However, several of the girls have turned from their Christian principles. One is living with a man to whom she is not married. Was this rebellion some sort of reaction to the home in which they lived, of resentment towards Grandmother Parrish's interference in their lives? Perhaps they are only now expressing what they must have felt many times at home and were unable to show.

Recently the grandmother died. Her death must have represented release from her demanding ways and unwise interference. At last, after 30 years, May and Russell Parrish know what privacy is in their marriage. Why did they put up with it so many years? Because the large old house belonged to the grandmother and her son was an only child. It was an even more difficult situation than having the widow live with her son. He and his wife and children were in reality living with grandmother.

What is the reason most often given for separation or divorce by the separating partners? In-law trouble. How often you have heard: "If my parents would have just left us alone, I think we might have made it." "She was always running home to mother about everything that happened." "He asked his parents' advice about everything without even considering me."

You have in your power the potential to utterly destroy your child's marriage. This is a lethal power and one that must be controlled and guarded constantly. One widow I know was not satisfied after her husband's death until she got her son to come home—without his wife! Oh, she would be shocked if you were to accuse her of breaking up the marriage, but the constant interference in her children's lives started an avalanche that no one could stop. She stood at the top of the hill and gave the kick it needed to get it going on its disastrous course.

When the day comes that I can no longer care for my own needs, I do not want to be moved into the home of one of my children. I could not bear the thought of being a hindrance in their lives or of interfering. Retirement homes and nursing homes are gaining in popularity. I would gladly enter one even though it would be less easy for me to be happy there rather than be a lodestone to my children and their families.

One elderly woman I know often tells her children, "Don't ever put me in a nursing home. I would kill myself before I would go to one." Life has a way of making us do the very thing we say adamantly we shall never do. It would not surprise me to hear some day that Mrs. Brown has had to be placed in a nursing home and I doubt very much that she would attempt to take her life when the possibility became reality.

There is no place where one's character is more evident than in a nursing home. The patterns of years of thought habits and attitudes are now quite apparent. Some older persons are gentle and sweet and thoughtful of those around them; others are cantankerous and difficult to get along with. Form the habit now of permitting a gracious spirit to rule your being and in the years ahead you will keep your friends' and family's love and respect.

Should you take your vacation with your married children? If your son or son-in-law has a time-consuming position and as a consequence sees little of his family, doubtless he will appreciate his two weeks alone with them. Remember, you are an outsider—no matter how much they protest and want you to come along. If, on the other hand, you live some distance from your children and do not see them often, spending a vacation together could prove beneficial to both you and them. But, if you decide to go along, determine to fit into their plans remembering that after all it is their hard-earned vacation time. Let them make the choices as to where to go, what to see, where to stop for overnight lodging, and where and when to eat. If you have low blood sugar, for instance, and must eat on time, do not belabor the point. Carry some crackers or fruit along so that you can nibble if it is necessary. Become a congenial traveler and flexible in fitting into their plans—without becoming noticeably quiet if choices are not yours. Look for something good to say about every place you visit and in case you cannot stand the food, don't be an embarrassment to your family by bawling out the waitress and sending your plate back to the kitchen. Make it a point to put up and shut up. Be positive. Let them know that you are having a great time and enjoying the trip immensely. Let them remember you as being such a good sport.

One of my most treasured moments is my small grandson Randy asking, "Isn't grandma going with us? Oh, gee, if she doesn't go along, we won't have any fun!" I am sure there have been times I have not earned or deserved this, but it my special aim to earn it every time I am with my grandchildren.

An even further reward is that you may be invited to go along again—not out of a sense of duty but because you are genuinely wanted.

I have learned that holidays are something I do not plunge into and take the initiative in planning. I wait to find out if the children have any plans and if none seems to be apparent, then I feel free to ask them to spend Christmas, New Year's, or whatever, with me. But I do not want them to feel it is imperative that they do so for every holiday. Nor shall I let myself feel offended if they make plans to be some place else when the day arrives. Should my daughter-in-law's parents feel they ought to spend the special holiday in her home, I shall remain flexible. I well remember in the early years of my marriage how torn we were when holidays came and both sides of our family felt we would, of course, spend the day in their home. We often ended up eating two Christmas dinners, one at noon and the other in the evening, in order to keep harmony and to avoid hurt feelings.

Christmas dinner doesn't have to be on Christmas Day. It can be equally as festive the day before, or even a week or so before.

As we discussed earlier, it is not easy adjusting to not being first in someone's life—but it is disastrous when a widow insists on assuming this position in her children's lives. God the loving Father wants to be first in your life. Give him that position. Let him be your first thought upon awakening and your last upon going to bed at night. St. Augustine wrote, "The soul is restless until it finds its rest in Thee." Know the perfect rest of depending upon him for your needs and for life itself. Practice his presence in your daily routine. When you awaken in the night, call upon him—and you will find him listening and never tiring of your prattle. Mark the verses in your Bible that bring special comfort such as II Timothy 1:7: "For God hath not given us the spirit of fear; but of power, and of love, and of a sound mind."

12

When the Grass Needs Mowing

Without a husband, a yard burgeons into twice or three times its size almost overnight. The grass grows much faster now that you are without a man to mow it. And in winter the sidewalks lengthen until there is much more snow to be shoveled than in former years.

At the first sign of grass to be mowed in the spring, I phoned a young neighbor and made arrangements for him to mow it. The result was a green-striped zebra. He failed to cut his rows closely enough and the result was unsightly. When I suggested that he run his mower over the missed portions of the rows, he was insulted, and although I paid him for the work, he went home in a less-than-friendly mood. His mother has seemed cooly distant ever since.

The second boy was some improvement at first. At least there were no rough seams of grass between his rows. But halfway through his motor stopped and he went home. Although I waited for several days he never returned to finish the job or to collect his money.

My third attempt to find a yard man was more success-

ful. A friend recommended the retiree who worked for
her, an 84-year-old gentleman of the old school who
charged by the hour. Mr. Rhodes not only knew how to
mow a lawn properly, but he knew how to trim the
bushes, paint the garage, put locks on the windows, repair the spring in the garage door, and more. You name it
and Mr. Rhodes could do it well. I only hope he lives to
be a hale and hearty 100!

Betty Curns, however, has been a widow for several
years and has had the same young yard boy for many
summers. Patiently she trained him to do the work she
wanted done and her patience has paid off well. He could
not tell a thistle from an aster when he first came to her,
but now has become very knowledgeable in the field of
botany — all because she encouraged him.

Another friend, who has a very large yard and formal
gardens discovered that a full-time gardener was hard to
find. So she makes use of the Salvation Army's work
program and has men work for her by the day all summer
long. Like Betty Curns she too has unusual patience and
some of the men she employs have been won from lives
of drunkenness. In establishing a fine work relationship
she has been of great help in reclaiming some of these
men for Christ.

She often works along with them and her beautiful
garden not only attests to her patience but also is enjoyed
by many people in the spring, summer, and fall.

When a woman cannot take care of her yard herself
she quite naturally must look a little harder at the question of whether or not she really wants to continue living
in that house. The answer may well be no. Then it is she
must study all the possibilities that are before her — an

apartment, condominium, townhouse, mobile home, or smaller house.

Each has its special benefits. The apartment eliminates not only yard work but maintenance problems, though she may have to wait for days to have the latter cared for if her landlord is lazy.

The condominium accomplishes the relief from maintenance and yard work as well, but here there is the danger of an ever-growing demand for funds for maintenance and other improvements which may be far more than rental increases would be. Also, the condominium is difficult to resell in most areas.

Choosing another home may be a difficult decision without a husband's help. As we discussed earlier, the house on the hilltop or the picturesque country cottage may be attractive but not practical for the widow who needs family and friends around her. A home from which she can easily walk to a shopping district, library, drugstore, hardware store, post office, without having to depend upon a car is ideal. Access to public transportation is also an important factor.

You may be wondering just what improvements you should make before you place your home on the market. What will help its sale? What will prove to be money down the drain? It may be wise to get expert advice here.

How about the bushes in front of your house? Are they badly overgrown and do they hide your front entrance and make it look more like a jungle than home? Here wise pruning may prove a decided asset to the sale of your house — without much expense involved.

The entrance to your home is all-important. Do the porch or steps need repair? Find someone to replace any split or broken boards in the steps or porch and see that both steps and porch are freshly painted.

If the front door has badly weathered, see that it is sanded, bleached, and revarnished or repainted in a complimentary color. Be sure that the locks work well and the door opens easily without the hinges squeaking.

Your entry hall is also of the utmost importance. Does the floor need retiling? Is the room dark and gloomy? Could new paint or wallpaper create a better atmosphere? See that this is done even if it means hiring someone else to do the work.

Salvation Army men are often adept at paper hanging and inside painting. If you live in a college town a call to the campus employment bureau often can provide you with quite skilled help.

The freshness of the drapes and curtains at all of the windows is also important to the overall appearance of your house. Here is something that you yourself can do to greatly aid in the attractiveness of your home.

The kitchen above all other rooms is important to the woman who is considering your house. This is one room that should be freshly painted and the wood cupboards cleaned with an efficient cleaner. Fresh house plants in the windows can add a lot to the attractiveness of your kitchen and dining areas.

The question of whether or not to paint your house before you put it up for sale depends upon how long it has been since it was last painted and what condition the paint is in. If it is peeling, by all means have your house and trim painted. If done within three months of selling, the cost of paint and labor may be deducted from your capital gains tax.

Painters must also be investigated before hiring them.

It is dangerous to pick names at random from the phone book. One woman I know who did this regretted the day the men set foot on her grounds. Not only were they expensive, they were also careless and sloppy. The appearance of the porch, after they finished, was so unsightly she finally had to hire another painter to scrape off the paint and repaint the wood. This time she called the Salvation Army and was pleased with the workman they sent her. It would have been much simpler, and less expensive, if the job had been done right in the first place.

Should you decide in favor of keeping your present home with its large yard, perhaps you should take another look at the types of shrubbery that line its borders. Are they planted in hard-to-care-for flowers and edgings? Now may be the time to find hardy plant varieties of evergreen. Evergreens are not inexpensive but are well worth the price of what they save in labor and add in beauty.

Such yard projects may serve more than one purpose in adding value to your property and aiding you in making the adjustment into widowhood. There is therapeutic value in working in your yard, perhaps planting a small vegetable garden that you can share with neighbors. There is both mental and spiritual healing for your tired mind and spirit not to mention the good to be realized by the exercise afforded your muscles.

New flowers in your yard may do much more for you than those on your husband's grave. One woman I know went to the cemetery every day with flowers. Both she and others would have benefited far more had she taken the flowers to shut-ins in nursing homes, or provided them for the Sunday services in her church. Cemeteries, fortunately, have rules about this sort of thing that serve to prevent overindulgence by the bereaved.

Although the marker bears your husband's name, do not think of him as being there. To remain close to your loved one is better accomplished by remaining close to God in prayer and through meditating on his Word.

Perhaps it is with you as it was with me: the grass in your pasture or lawn needs mowing. There is no one in sight to mow it for you. You have a health problem and cannot. Your son is working and barely has time to mow his own lawn. The young boys in the vicinity seem more interested in Little League. Their allowances are so large they do not see the need for earning money.

God knows all about pastures — and lawns, too. He knows about grass that withers and dies, but in the meantime needs cutting. You can trust him to solve all of your problems — even when it is mowing the lawn. And when *you* are the grass, he is still to be trusted. His cutting blade is sharp and his mowing is sure.

13

How to Be a Fifth Wheel and Like It

One of the most difficult adjustments a widow makes is in the area of social life. The cheery "Can you and your husband come for barbecue tomorrow night?" that once accompanied the ringing of the phone is seldom heard as couples the two of you once enjoyed look elsewhere for a foursome. This is especially true when the axis of friendship was between the men.

At a time in your life when you most need the support of old friends, they suddenly are just not there. It's common for people to avoid trouble and flee from sorrow and pain. C. S. Lewis, in *A Grief Observed*, written after his wife's death from cancer, said friends crossed the street to avoid having to greet him.

Fortunately there are still women friends of long standing who out of sympathy will ply you with dinner engagements. How long the invitations continue will greatly depend upon you.

No one wants a dinner guest who is teary-eyed, who talks on at length of her husband this and her husband that. I can think of one acquaintance who has worn out her welcome with many friends because she talks incessantly of the things she and her husband did together — and he's been dead 10 years!

You may need to relearn the art of conversation, which consists of being a good listener and introducing into the conversation items of genuine interest to your listeners. For even though you may think otherwise, life is still going on. Be genuinely interested in the other person, his or her dreams and goals, past experiences. Ask discreet questions that keep him talking.

One of the things I missed most about my husband was his commentary on the news. I depended upon him for political insight. I find now that I myself must study the political scene and keep abreast of the main things that are happening in local, state, national, and world affairs. I find that I am enjoying the knowledge I am accumulating.

Discipline yourself to be interested in crewel work, water color, oil painting, in the Old Masters, macramé, hanging plants, or in whatever your friend is interested. Ask questions and show genuine appreciation.

Join a Great Books Club; haunt your local library; spend the time you used to spend doing things with your husband in your own self-improvement. If you have ever had an interest in writing, become a member of a writers' club and attend a summer writers' conference.

Sign up for classes in your local junior college for credit or for audition. Become acquainted with the thinking of the younger generation. Don't let yourself be addicted to the "my generation" type of philosophy.

Discretion is the word. Avoid like the plague being placed in a situation that would cause you to look anything but cooly disinterested in your friend's mate. The green-eyed monster thrives on fifth-wheelers. They are at the very top of his list. You will find that where once in the presence of your husband you could banter conversation lightly and facetiously across the net, you are now a "threat" to your married women friends. Even though you know you could never give a serious thought to another man, his wife does not know this.

"Avoid even the appearance of evil" is just as sound advice now as it was in Bible times. Do not permit a friend's husband to come to your home alone for any reason — to unclog the kitchen drain, to watch his favorite program on TV when their set is broken, to eat a meal when she is out of town or whatever. If he comes on the pretext to watch TV, for example, find an errand that will take you out of the house while he is there if necessary. This simple little rule can save much grief and many a desirable friendship.

Monitor your words. For example, do not single out your friend's husband to compliment him on how good he is looking in his new suit; instead, wisely include both the wife and husband in your compliment.

I found myself in the living room visiting with the man while the wife was in the kitchen preparing to serve dinner. I had never particularly liked to visit with this man in the past, but there was deep within me a real need for "male conversation." Afterwards I realized my timing was wrong. I should have helped my friend in the kitchen and saved my questions for the dinner hour, or the demitasse later when both could be included. It is important in being a good third or fifth wheel to keep your focal point on the wife and not on her mate.

And if you should find yourself alone with a married man be sure to turn the conversation around to his wife

with such complimentary expressions as how wise he
was to have married a woman like her. Never let him use
you as a mop-up for any complaints he may have about
his wife.

If the affections of the widow or divorcee are to be
kept harnessed and under the rein of the Holy Spirit, God
must be allowed to fill the gap.

People like to be with people who are happy. Smooth
out the depressions in your life. It helps to spend time out
of doors in the sunshine. Warm sunshine is a good healer
for emotional depression. Tears dry up in the warm sun
and evaporate. Learn to sing again! "Laugh and the
world laughs with you." "Now the God of hope fill you
with all joy and peace in believing, that ye may abound in
hope, through the power of the Holy Ghost " (Romans
16:15).When you learn to be a part of his joy you will not
mind being a fifth wheel.

Make yourself attractive. If you are overweight, see
your doctor and ask him for a special diet. Dieting is
really a simple matter of figuring out how many calories
you need each day and remaining within that limit, or
below. It doesn't matter whether you eat calories in the
early morning or in the middle of the night.

After you have slimmed down, go through your ward-
robe. Purchase some new clothes. Avoid dark colors:
buy perky combinations of jackets, blouses, and skirts.

Proper exercise can do a lot for your figure and your
state of mind. Join the YWCA in your town and benefit
by gym classes, folk dancing and the swimming it offers.
Bicycling is good for the circulation and so is walking —
the most available and least expensive form of exercise.
Leave your car at home on short errands.

Spend some time and thought on your hair and skin.

Find a good beauty operator; sometimes a woman working in her home will prove less expensive and give you more individual attention than the run-of-the-mill beauty shop. As for your skin, remember the strong sun is not for the older woman. Avoid that leathery, thick-skinned look some women who have been sunworshippers, golfers, or swimmers in their younger days acquire as they grow older. Brimmed hats are back in style so wear one when you bicycle or are going to be in the sun for long.

Take good care of your skin. Cleanse it regularly with a good soap and water and keep it generously treated with a good moisturizer. Avoid the expensive heavy creams put out by cosmetic companies at ridiculous prices. Many are of no help. Some of the purest skin aids are to be found in your own kitchen: oatmeal masks, avocado and honey for nourishment, egg yolk for an astringent mask.

The best moisturizers are to be found in health food stores where you can be sure they're pure and contain the added beneficial vitamins they advocate.

When you become a happy person, not with a surface act, but with a happiness that swells up inside you from being in harmony with God and his creation, you will find you no longer mind being a fifth wheel because you know in your heart this is God's choosing for you. And you will know that he intends his joy to be yours.

> Let no man destroy my joy, today
>   This redbird that sang here inside
>   only yesterday,
>   let it sing and soar today.
> Let no jack-in-the-box despair

           clip its wings,
           turn it into raven, crow
           to haunt some farmer's field
           portending gloom.
       Let these bright red wings
           tint a cloud,
           chase a rainbow
           across a rain-clear sky,
       And when evening falls
           let their deepening wings
           soft-flutter, nest upon a star.

". . .neither be ye sorry; for the joy of the Lord is your
strength " (Nehemiah 8:10).

14

God Never
Makes Junk

The humorist Erma Bombeck once wrote in her syndicated column, "God never makes junk." This succinct statement contains a startling truth that you, when the adversary comes to tempt you and make you think you are nothing, would do well to remind yourself of. Realize that you are a part of his creation. The Psalmist writes, "He made us and not we ourselves. . ."

God intended all of his children to be beautiful. Babies start out beautiful—but life has a way of corrupting and effacing the person God made in his image. The Son of God came to do away with the corrupting and the effacing, once and for all. Would he have suffered the death on the cross, the shame and debasement, for *nothing*? Indeed not. He had far more important things to do in keeping his universe in order. When he took time out from reining in the stars, and planting new galaxies, it had to be an important business priority. His death on the cross was just that, a spiritual priority in the battle for the souls of his created men and women.

One of the peculiar mental hang-ups that often faces

the widow in adjusting to reality is the feeling of worth-lessness. "What good am I?" "What can I do?" "Why should I be left and James taken?" "I am nothing!"

I have just come from the mobile home of one of the women in our mobile court who lost her husband six months ago and is suffering a deep depression accompanied by extreme apathy from which she is unable so far to extricate herself. Her marriage had been an intrinsic marriage. They had done everything together. She kept the books for his business. When he sailed his boat, she went along. When she went to the store, he went with her. She had no interests separate from his. The adjustment to living alone after such a close comradeship is much more difficult than when the wife has had interests of her own. If perhaps the husband's business interests have made such demands on his time that his wife has been forced to develop interests of her own, these prove most helpful when it becomes necessary for her to live without her mate.

What could I say to Marcia Hendrix? What she wanted was her husband alive again. She cried out, "I just can't accept it! I just can't accept it!" She had no choice in the matter. As long as she lives in this world, her husband is not going to return to her.

I reminded her that she would find the adjustment easier once she accepts the fact of her husband's death. "God has his reasons for taking James home. . ."

"I no longer believe in God!" she screamed. Here was a woman who in her younger days had considered going as a missionary. Now in the agony of her grief she disclaimed any belief in her Maker.

"You do not mean that, Marcia," I told her, "you are angry at everything and at God for allowing James to die, and that is why you are lashing out at God with such statements.''

In her distraught state, there was not too much I could tell her and I knew she needed someone to simply listen to her talk. There was much rumination—"I don't know what to do!" she repeated time after time, shaking her head dejectedly.

My heart went out to her for I knew I had never known the depths of her despair. In the agony of my grief although it had put me in a state of limbo for days, I never doubted God nor his higher purpose in my grief. Like the words of the popular gospel song, "He was there all the time! He was there all the time!"

Marcia was a two year old having a mental tantrum on the floor of her despair. She was kicking and screaming in her agony and anger. I listened to her mental tirade. But I knew in my heart there is very little anyone can do for Marcia until she comes to grip with the spiritual battle she is fighting and yields her life to Christ.

"I can't do anything," she moaned.

"Oh, but you can and you are," I told her. "You have filled out all of your estate papers and are getting your legal matters in order. Many woman in your condition couldn't possibly take care of so many difficult details." At this she perked up. "Do you think there is something I can do?" she asked.

"Of course, there are many things you can do. You are an attractive woman with a background in business. When the time comes, you will find some place to make a contribution."

"Do you think I could be a nurse's aid in the hospital?"

"Yes," I told her, "they are so needed."

Why did her faith fail her when she needed it, I wondered? But I knew the answer in my own heart. She had failed to keep her house of faith in order before the disaster struck and the straws of indifference she had used for the foundation just could not stand against the hurricane. Now, she will have to start out on the bare rock—the rock Christ Jesus—and build from scratch.

In June Filkin Taylor's beautiful book, *But for Our Grief*, she tells how her faith grew in calmness and serenity as she looked to the Bible for comfort after the sudden death of her small daughter. She writes that Jeremiah 32:42 and Job 5:17-18 show her that God is not surprised by any of our troubles. "He hurts with us and longs for us to grow and respond His way, but there is nothing in our lives that He doesn't permit. Now I think I can say with Paul Tournier, 'What I have to do is to put my signature at the foot of a blank page in which I will accept whatever God wishes to write. I cannot predict what He will put on this blank Contract as my life proceeds—but I give my signature today.' "

When the loss of a loved one comes to someone who has signed, or is willing to sign, such a blank page with God, the grief is far less devastating, and the adjustment to living is far more simple. Marcia is typical of the thousands who must face grief without the arm of the Lord to sustain them. Such a position can be most devastating.

For the believing Christian, weak or strong, grief is invariably a time of testing. Like Job, he finds himself or herself thwarted by Satan and buffeted in many different ways. Satan is wily and knows when we are weak. Then it is he moves in with all of his forces and tempts us to cast ourselves down the mountainside and to turn our backs on God. "Look what he has done to your husband after all of the years your husband served him so faithfully! Do you want to keep on singing the praises of such a God?" When these dark thoughts come, we need to rebuke Satan as we are instructed to do in the New Testament—and, God tells us, "he will flee from you!"

The other day while waiting at the meat counter, I got to talking to a young woman who asked me, "What makes you so happy?"

"I've just had my book accepted by a publisher for publication," I told her.

"You have! What's the title?" she asked me.

"Well, I call it, *Without a Man in the House*, but I don't know what it will finally be titled."

"Is it a book about widows?" she asked me.

"Yes, widowssand other women who are left without husbands."

"Oh, I want to read it," she exclaimed. "My husband travels overseas all the time and I just know I am going to end up being a widow and I want to be prepared for it."

I was a little startled by her response, but after I thought about it, I thought she was wise in being prepared. Some years ago a man wrote a book called, *Prepare Your Wife to be a Widow*. Nothing a man does in life can be much more important than for him to consider what will happen to his wife when death takes him, but few men have the forethought or are willing to face up to the starkness of such a thought to do anything about it. Many neglect to set their legal matters in order by the simple making of a will.

The runner/preacher Bobbie Richardson once prayed in a public meeting: "Dear Lord, Your will. Nothing more. Nothing less. Amen."

This simple prayer can bring much comfort to the heart of the widow. The knowledge that God is working in your life and has not turned his back on you even though your social life has completely changed is strength-giving. In his Word he has said, "For now your creator will be your husband. . ." (Isaiah 54:5a, *Jerusalem Bible*).

There are many evidences of his serving as "my husband" in my life. I enjoy looking for the eviences of his love and care for my well being. One immediate example came to my mind as I returned to Monet Acres this year. I knew the frost last year had seriously damaged some of the plants around my mobile home. I dreaded seeing the brown shriveled leaves on the euphoria hedge and the three dead palm trees that edged my lot. I took a special delight in these small trees. But the killing cold had taken them as it had many trees in southern Florida.

To my amazement as I drove into the drive, I saw that neither hedge nor palms were in evidence. My neighbors who had arrived two weeks earlier had removed them so that I would not have that worry. God was "being a husband" to me! Digging them up would have been an impossibility for me. I often find in areas where things are impossibilities, God takes over and sees that the impossibilities are cared for. Thank You, dear Heavenly Father!

Among the many problems I inherited as a result of my husband's traumatic illness was an old farm house. I had looked at it many times during the years and wondered how in the world my husband was going to renovate it and make it liveable.

When the house became my singular dilemma, the impossibilities loomed even larger for I could not hammer a nail or cope with the sagging floors, crooked walls, mis-hung doors, and the ancient wavy shake-covered roof.

These obvious faults were multipled by loose plaster on several of the ceilings, and a gaping hole a foot square in the brick foundation.

"Sell it! Or, better still, burn it down!" This was the advice of well intentioned friends. But I was strapped with it because in the forming of the trust, of which I was trustee, the farm had been placed in the "A" of the "A-B" Trust and I could not sell the "A" portion of the trust in my lifetime.

If I had had unlimited funds, there would have been no problem in calling in workmen and having the job done professionally, but this I could not afford.

When the encephalitis struck, my husband had been working in the basement on the sick foundation and the sagging floors. His tools were scattered on the basement floor just as he had left them. I did not even know what many were intended for. He had purchased an old drum-type cement mixer and intended to repair the foundation wall himself.

The situation was listed high on my list of "impossibilities." I asked my yard man to look at it. He took one look at the gaping hole and backed away exclaiming, "I wouldn't touch it with a ten-foot pole!"

For months I despaired of ever fixing the aperture, but the bricks continued to loosen and to fall and I realized I must solve the problem. I decided to discuss the problem with a Christian man who had repaired a plaster problem in our house. He was used to working with brick and mortar and knew just what to do. He said he would need about 100 bricks which my daughter and I hauled from a local brick yard. I know God had provided Mr. Schram to meet my impossibility.

I never cease to be amazed how the Lord has solved the many impossible repair problems at the farm. Some months before his illness, my husband had purchased antique brick veneer siding to use in the kitchen and entry way. For months it had been stacked in unopened boxes in the store room adjacent to the kitchen.

Who would have thought God would send a 12-year-old girl, a 14-year-old boy and two "rascals," eight and five, to brick the kitchen wall! But that is what happened. I spent two weeks at the farm with my four grandchildren who were in my care while their parents were on a speaking tour to California. I would not have had the nerve to violate child labor laws by asking these children to work on the old farmhouse, but to my amazement I found they considered it a great lark—and a challenge.

Autumn was upon us and I did not want to have to heat the farm house or the trailer during the winter months. Reminding God of his promise to be "my husband," I placed a 3 x 5 card advertising the trailer on the bulletin board in the nearby bank foyer.

I had no trouble finding a renter for the trailer. But the house lacked so much in the way of repairs that I did not have the heart to advertise it. However, the Lord understood. One day a young man called to inquire about the trailer. I told him it was rented and hearing his disappointment I said, "Would you be interested in renting a farm house that is in need of repair?" He had just sold his house and had to move right away and was pleased to find a place where he could have a work credit for part of the rent.

The Lord foresaw the hazards I did not even know existed. In replacing the floor covering in the bathroom, my new renter discovered the floor had rotted out and he ended up replacing floor, ceiling, walls, tub, stool and lavoratory! The cost of the fixtures and tiling was mine, of course, but it was much cheaper than if I had to have outside workmen come in.

We can trust God with far more than our spiritual needs. He is able to meet our physical and material needs as well.

When we have done all that we can do within the scope of our limitations, (and sometimes what may seem to us a little beyond) God is there with his unlimited resources, ready to step in and provide our needs. He is not a limited yard man who looks at the task and says he will not touch it with a 10-foot pole. He is, if that is what is needed, the skilled bricklayer who can rebuild our walls and the gaping holes in our foundations, and provide work-oriented renters for the empty farm houses of our lives.

We are important to God. He proves it often not by the great giant answers to our garguantuan prayers, but by the answers to our small night cries.

Although he may be concerned with galaxy on galaxy, he is never too occupied to hear his children when they call his name.

15

Decisions, Decisions

You probably were not aware of all the decisions that were entailed in living when your huband was there to make them for you. But now, after years of having his help in every decision from what color rug to buy for the living room to what make and model car, you find you are having to make all decisions alone. This can be an emotional trauma.

Although I had had many years of experience in the business world, I was appalled to find how much I had depended upon my husband for the many decisions involved in day-to-day living.

Because he abhorred shopping for himself I often selected his clothing for him. But I liked to have him with me when I chose my dresses, coats, and other wearing apparel. For some reason, I always liked the things he preferred. He had a good eye for fit and color.

So here was a vulnerable area for me. I had a relative help me in the first dress I bought after my husband's illness. She persuaded me to buy a gray knitted two-piece dress which was an utter mistake. As soon as I got it home, I realized it was not my style and I would never wear it. Both the color and the knit were for a younger person. Instead of flattering, it accentuated the salt and pepper in my hair and the bulges in my waistline.

If you have always been dependent upon your husband for the many decisions necessary in living, as I found I had been, then you are in for problems in this area. Or if yours was a marriage where your husband made all decisions, ranging from supper menus to vacation plans, doubtless you are finding yourself in deep waters.

The tendency is to transfer your leaning to someone else's shoulders. This can prove disastrous for none of these relationships is as close as was that between you and your husband. No matter how dear, these people do not know you as well as he did. They are not able to make as beneficial decisions where your welfare is concerned.

My son, concerned over my being alone in our large house, gave me a red Irish setter named Sewanee. Sewanee was a puppy — an expensive purchase for my son as he had a pedigree — and this little puppy was to keep me company and serve as a watch dog.

Well, he was not good company for he kept me awake nights (and the neighbors as well, I'm afraid) and he would have welcomed anyone who wanted to get in! On top of all that, he was not house-trained. In those first weeks of my husband's illness the last thing I needed was a puppy to house-train.

Ever since then, when I find myself being prodded into a questionable decision by some well-meaning friend or relative I whisper to myself "remember Sewanee!" If nothing else, he has actually saved me from many needless expenditures.

Sometimes when you have arrived at a decision you may find it is one that is not readily accepted by your family and friends. Remember the verse, "wise is the man [or woman] who keeps his [or her] own counsel." This word from Proverbs is important to you now when so many, often quite surprisingly, are making your business their business.

Listen attentively and gratefully to all of the advice that comes your way but after praying about it when you are alone, do exactly as you feel God would have you do.

Take a pencil and paper and write down the pros and cons of what you are trying to decide. Often you will find one very strong pro that will make the decision easier, or a strong con that will let you know it would be unwise.

In addition to making a list of pros and cons there are other questions it would be well to ask yourself.

1. Is the decision in accord with biblical teachings?
2. Will it adversely affect anyone—particularly family or friends?
3. Can I afford it?
4. Is the purchase, trip, or whatever, necessary or desirable?
5. Whom will it benefit? Myself? Others? No one?
6. Is it in the will of God? His direct will? Or his permissive will?
7. Will the decision further the work of our Lord?
8. Is there another choice that could prove to be superior?

There are Scripture verses that can help in decision-making. "And when he putteth forth is own sheep, he goeth before them, and the sheep follow him: for they know his voice" (John 10:4).

When you are faced with a decision you do not seem to be able to make with assurance don't make it. There may be some very good reason why you should not at the time. Pray about it and look to the Lord until you have what you feel is His leading for you. Does this apply even to small matters like dresses, purses, etc.? Yes, nothing is too small or insignificant to be taken to the Lord in prayer. He welcomes you at any time of the day or night.

Of course, decisions need to be tempered by circumstances and good common sense. For example, if you are in need of a storm door before winter comes, and your local hardware store is advertising a sale on storm doors, don't expect the Lord to send handwriting on the wall.

I once knew a farmer who waited all fall for the Lord to give him direction to harvest his corn. Day after day he prayed, but no answer came. Christmas found him with his corn standing in the field. Mr. Spackly should have known that God expects us to use the common sense he gave us and gone out into his fields with his machinery in high gear. But his desire for a sign in the sky — or wherever — brought ill to himself, his church, and his Christian testimony in the eyes of his neighbors.

If you have made a wrong or hasty decision do not become depressed over it. Chalk it up to experience and let it be a safe-guard in future decision-making. Remember you are not perfect — no one is. There are bound to be some times when you make the wrong decisions.

There are people who seem to make the right decision all of the time, but that is because you do not know about the wrong decisions they make. Wrong decisions are a part of living and you are entitled to your share.

Close the door firmly to the house you have sold, to

the car, to the trailer, to the TV, and don't regret the selling. Refuse to play Lot's wife. Looking back on a decision, a transaction, or a deed and allowing yourself to feel remorse or regret can actually turn you into an immovable statue where future decision-making is concerned.

When we left our first home to go into the Lord's work in a distant city, we had to sell most of our furniture. I felt badly over parting with a maple table that had been in my childhood home. My husband said, "Never let yourself become attached to sticks and stones. They are not worthy of our deep feelings." Since then I have had many tables to be preferred over that one — and I think of his words whenever it is time to part with an object that has served me well.

Green grass in other meadows than our own often seems more inviting, but we need to be sure before we wander over the fence that it is God's time for us to move on.

This verse in Psalms is most interesting for it is almost the reverse of what we may think is God's way in our lives: "Man chooseth the path that he will take, but God directs His steps." Apparently we have the power of choice, but God is concerned about our daily living and the very steps we take. Watch for his little unobtrusive arrows on your way. Yesterday I mentioned to a friend my desire to own a bicycle, even though such an investment seemed foolish for something I would be using only two or three months in the year. "Oh," she answered, "my husband has a bike he never uses." She later brought it over and to my delight I found it to be one I could ride easily. Thank you, Lord!

How can you know the will of God in your life? There

are three questions to bear in mind and when the answers all agree you can feel certain.

1. Are there apparent circumstances through which God is leading?
2. Do spiritual friends concur with your course of action?
3. Do you have an inner assurance that you are in His will? A feeling of peace backed up by Scripture?

16

Petticoat Plumbing

"Whatever in the world would you do without me?" the voice was loving but at the same time edged with some disgust. Disgust at my complete ineptitude where mechanical things were concerned. I had put the key to the night lock in upside down and it had lodged there waiting for my husband to extricate it.

He often told me he didn't know how anyone could be born as completely lacking in mechanical ability as I had been. I merely shrugged my shoulders and continued to direct all of the needed repairs in our house to him. His skill made me seem even more helpless by comparison. But it was a helplessness life was not going to let me luxuriate in the rest of my years.

After some months of living alone, I have to admit that I am not quite as helpless as I made my husband think. Part of it had been a clinging vine act. Still, a very large part of it was for real.

The kitchen sink has always been a problem in my married life, probably because we have always lived in old houses with antiquated plumbing. It was a problem that had a way of raising its hooded cobra head on holidays when I was in the midst of cooking a dinner for family and guests. My husband spent part of many holidays under the kitchen sink.

Plumbing can be a major problem for the woman living alone. Consequently, I diligently poured soda into the drain every week or two and for almost two years I was free of drainage problems. But then the inevitable happened. Following a drastic drop to a record 22 below-zero, I awoke one morning to find the drain in the kitchen sinks plugged.

Believing the problem to be a frozen pipe, I tried to be ingenious in thinking of methods to open it. Running hot water did not help. I tried wrapping a heating pad around what I hoped was the frozen drain pipe in the basement. This didn't help either.

A search of the grocer shelves disclosed a new type of crystals. I followed directions carefully, but nothing happened. Discouraged, I went to bed hoping a miracle such as a freak January thaw would happen during the night. But morning came with the same brackish water standing in the double sinks.

The drug store shelf had a new "plunger-type" drain opener. I purchased one even though it cautioned it should not be employed if any of the lye-type drain openers had previously been used or if the sink were a double one.

I thought I could solve the double-sink problem by plugging a wet towel into the drain of one sink and holding it in place while I plunged the plunger into the drain opening on the other side. The explosion that resulted was far more than I could control with my hand held over the towel. Black water shot five feet into the air, ruining the white curtains and streaking my wall and windows with ugly black rivulets of sewer water.

In the middle of my Hiroshima, the front door bell rang, and, grabbing a towel to wipe the black spots that had splashed on my blouse, arms and glasses (thanking the Lord for the glasses!) I hurried to extend hospitality to the young couple and child I found waiting on the front porch. One of my husband's former students who was home on furlough from a mission term in Australia had decided to drop by with her husband and young child. Delighted to see them, I ushered them into the living room and closed the door to the fume-filled kitchen.

After their visit, I marched back into the kitchen ready for action. The problem as I saw it was that the force from the power plunger was dissipated by the second drain. I replaced the sink drainer, plugged the wet towel securely over the drain, and then placed a stainless steel lid over the towel. Climbing upon the counter, and holding the lid in place with one foot, I leaned over the sink and gave the plunger a quick sharp downward shove. Even my weight on the lid was not sufficient. It rocked and some of the black water shot up my leg. But all was not lost—for suddenly the water in the sink gurgled noisily and disappeared. The drain was open!

The cost of the two drain openers amounted to $3.15 and the new curtains added up to just under $10 which was still considerably cheaper than $40 for the plumber.

In sewing up the new curtains, I ran into another problem. I had never needed a repair man for the sewing machine before. Always my husband could keep it operating smoothly. Now the shuttle came out and refused to go back into place. About to give up and call in a repair man, I discovered the manual in one of the drawers. Laboriously I studied the illustrations and after two unsuccessful attempts finally succeeded in getting the bobbin and shuttle securely into place and the curtains hemmed.

Shortly after my husband's illness, I called a plumber to check what I thought was a problem in the bathroom upstairs. The kitchen ceiling had had to be replastered where the lavatory had overflowed, but I could not tell if my husband had taken care of the problem before his illness or not. The plumber I called told me I was in serious trouble and that it would cost $400 to replace the pipes leading into the upstairs bathroom.

Shocked at his estimate, I called in a plumber a friend had recommended. He checked the pipes and said there was no present problem but because the plumbing was old there could be a problem in the future. He did not charge me for his visit and said he would include it at a future time if I needed him.

Recently, I awoke to find, after a five-inch downpour, that my basement had two inches of water. A quick check of outside drains revealed that one in the back of the house had become detached and that torrents of water were pouring from the roof into the ground by the foundation.

Rushing heedlessly into the cold rain, I managed to replace the drain pipe temporarily and to soak my new hair-do. I immediately called plumber number two. And he came to unclog the problem drain, and the water problem was solved. The charge was $38, but it was well worth it for I had no way of knowing how high the water would rise, or what damage it might do. I have since had the drain pipe securely and permanently fastened in place so that the problem cannot re-occur.

Lesson learned: check gutters for leaves and drain pipes to be sure they are functioning in minor rains so you will not be caught with clogged drains in a major downpour. Also, you cannot always trust the yellow pages of the phone book. To call in a plumber on a tic-tac-toe, round-we-go basis is only inviting trouble and high prices. Check with friends to find reliable workmen. If you must try out your own petticoat plumbing remember: when you rush out into the rain, put a plastic hood over your head and tie it securely!

I never cease to be amazed at some of the strange answers God sends to prayer. One cold windy October day, I took my three grandchildren to the farm to gather Jonathan apples for the cider press. It was after noon when we arrived at the farm house and hunger pangs caused us to become very impatient when the key failed to work in the lock. Twelve-year-old Missy took turns with me trying to get the lock to yield. It proved to be stubborn. Both of us were about to give up when eight-year-old Joel asked, "Why don't we pray about it?"

It was evident prayer was the only thing that was going to open the lock. As we raised our heads from praying, my attention was caught by a fat spider crawling rapidly across the door towards my hand. In a quick reflex action, I pulled the key from the lock and plunged it into his fat body. We cringed at the oozy mess it made. Trying the key once more, the lock yielded as though by magic—just the right lubrication! I can imagine our guardian angels were no less amused at the incident. We laughed together to think that God can even send spiders when we need them! Who would ever dream of *needing* a spider!

The plumber came shortly after the spider incident and

I examined the new pump he had put on the well and the new pipe he had added to reach the lower supply of water. We discussed the fact that still there was no water in the water line to the trailer. Neither of us had any idea where the water line had been placed and the use of a back-hoe could prove to be a difficult job when no one knew where the water line was.

He took a blunt instrument and knocked away at the corrosion. All of a sudden he was rewarded with a sudden spurt of water gushing from the pipe. Success! God not only uses spiders, but he uses people, too!

When I left my Florida trailer last March, I left with a sluggish drain in the kitchen. I knew I would need to call in a plumber when I returned this winter and I dreaded the expense. God, I am sure, has a very special place in his heart for women who must face problems alone. When I turned the water on, I was pleased to discover there was no sluggishness in evidence. The pipes were clear!

When you are plagued by plumbing problems, do not expect to be able to solve all of them. There are times when petticoat plumbing is not sufficient, and you will need a good plumber. There will be times when the answer to your plumbing prayers is in the form of a plumber skilled in his craft. God can lead you to the right person—if you will let him.

17

Of Boots, Zippers and Other Contrary Things

I knew there was some reason why I had not worn the boots all winter, some reason why I had not brought them down from the attic with the rest of the winter things. But in the six A.M. scramble to catch an early train in igloo land, I could not remember the reason. . .only the fact that there was a reason.

In my haste, one of the boots dropped on the attic stairs and sounded out a leather version of morning taps. Knee high, they were hard to get on, but I yanked and pulled, grateful for the feel of their warm sheep skin lining.

"Seven below with a chill factor of minus 37," the voice of the announcer groaned from my bedside radio. What a day to have to go into the city!

I tugged at a stubborn zipper. It yielded suddenly only to stop again stuck at mid-calf. That five pounds I gained over the holidays must have settled in my legs, I thought ruefully. I decided to leave the zipper at half mast—a forced decision because it would move neither up nor down. No matter, no one would know beneath my pant suit.

An hour later found me playing lineman with the commuter crowd at the station. I made a first down and settled by a window seat in the warm train. A glance down at the rounded toe of my boot suddenly brought a flash of recall: "These are the boots you can't get off!"

I remembered the last time I had worn them. I had had to keep them on all afternoon and evening until my husband returned from a late meeting in the city. What a picture I must have made welcoming him in my nightgown and boots—and that was before Marabel Morgan's *Total Woman* gave advice on novel ways to greet your husband.

"Don't ever wear these stupid things again!" he had admonished, his face red from the hard struggle of removing them.

Fortunately, there were other women at the luncheon who, because of the bitter cold, kept their boots on, too. I was glad for a place to hide the monsters under the table.

Back home again and inside my igloo with my heavy artillery, I tried to remove them, but found it was impossible. Among the many adjustments to living alone has been the zipper. I solved the can't-be-reached zipper in the back of dresses by wearing jackets when the occasion demanded, and selecting dresses that did not have back zippers, but a stuck zipper in a boot was something else again.

Problem: How to get the boots off? Carefully, I considered the solutions: One, to ask my son to drive over from the next town. On a cold winter night? Surely his wife, sweet as she was, could not help thinking, "Your mother isn't going to ask you to go out on a night like this just to help her get her boots off!''

Two, phone my good neighbor. And appear utterly ridiculous in his eyes. I could hear his children giggling over that eccentric Mrs. Burton.

Three, how about the police? That's what they're here for—to help people in trouble—or so I told myself. And have the call published in the local paper so the whole town would know about my boots?

My son-in-law phoned in the middle of my dilemma. He thought the situation hilarious and that I was being facetious when I suggested he might drive past on his way to work in the morning. Sleeping with my boots on. . .I tried lying down on the sofa in the TV room. I rebelled at the thought of spending the entire night in such discomfort.

Well, then, maybe a taxi? I could imagine myself frumping, "Oh, no, I don't want to go anywhere, I just want you to come inside and. . ." the driver would probably gun his motor in a fast get-away before I could explain about the boots.

My sense of humor is strictly a summer creature. It prefers to hibernate in the middle of winter. It disappears entirely into its cave with ice and snow and cars that won't start. . .and also with boots that won't come off.

I hunkered down on the stairs by the phone. Any feelings I had once fostered about Women's Lib had dimmed. Suddenly I was bolstered to an upright position—by the feel of the step beneath my hand. A flashback to my childhood and the rubbers my mother always made me wear at the slightest sprinkle. I used to pull them off on the rung of the chair, or the step, whichever was convenient. I pushed one boot against the riser and caught my heel firmly under the overhang. Hurrah! Boot number one came off with a loud thud.

But number two was more stubborn because of the zipper. I stood up for better leverage. The stair creaked and the leather moaned, but at last the heavy zipper yielded to the pull—and Women's Lib won another minor victory. Every woman needs to be as independent as possible not only from male domination, but from dependence upon male help.

Please never count me among those noble souls who want to be buried with their boots on. I am just not that noble. Oh, by the way, anyone need a pair of boots? Size seven. . .very warm, and very heavy.

18

Living Alone
and Transportation

In the majority of households the man assumes all or most of the responsibility for seeing that the family automobile is kept in proper running condition. A woman left alone may find the burden almost overwhelming.

The woman who knows how to drive has a decided advantage over the woman who has never driven a car or who gave up driving when she married. A car does give a woman a special independence, and owning and driving one can bring much happiness into her life as well as a lot of mechanical responsibility and at times headaches.

Where a man versed in mechanics can put up with an older car and keep it in good running order, the woman so gifted is rare. She will soon find an older car with its increasing maintenance and repair needs a real problem as well as a drain on her finances.

I became responsible for two cars — a late model Pinto station wagon and an older Pontiac LeMans. Since I did not need, and could not simultaneously drive, two cars, I decided to keep the newer Pinto and sell the Pontiac to my son. However the Pinto did not have power steering and this proved a real problem. The garage door came down on my head in a strong wind and caused an injury to an upper vertebra. While I had not minded doing without power steering before the accident, driving now became a very painful process without it. I lost sleep at night because of the pain in my back and shoulders.

I chose to sell the Pinto and purchased an eight-year-old Cadillac for a very low price. This proved to have both a good and a bad side. The car was a dream to drive and it was not long before my back was entirely healed; but the poor mileage made it very expensive—especially since I drove 23,000 miles in the year I owned it. That plus the $800 I paid out that year to have the brakes relined, a new muffler and exhaust system, a new radiator, a new alternator, new cables to the battery, a new starter, a right front wheel bearing, and the air conditioner repaired.

The car had been represented to me as having only 41,000 miles on it — and since I purchased it from a retired couple I thought it possible that they did not do much driving. However, as maintenance bills mounted I came to realize that the 41,000 miles on the car's odometer was not the whole story. As one mechanic pointed out, the car had possibly turned over the 100,000 mark and was on the second 100,000.

That sweet, quiet couple from whom I had purchased the car had remained extremely quiet and did not admit the hidden mileage even when I asked if the odometer was correct!

If I had thought the car had 141,000 miles on it I would not have considered it, but I still feel the car was the Lord's provision. When I divide the 23,000 miles into the cost of the car, the cost of maintenance and the cost of gas and oil, I find the year's cost a little over 12 cents a mile. In light of the 33 cents a mile that government estimates put on new cars, this was not too bad.

After 23,000 miles I was faced with replacing all four tires at once. I felt it was time not only to re-tire, but to consider purchasing a different car, for I had been stranded several times with this one.

The purchase of a new car was an almost traumatic experience for me. But spending such a large amount of money at one time made a real hole in my savings. I made a thorough study of the field and was fortunate to have a son-in-law whose brother was an electronics expert and could "talk cars" day and night without being bored.

Since gasoline economy has become a national issue I felt I could not conscientiously purchase another gas guzzler. I was disillusioned by the poor gas mileage on American-made cars. But I found I had an almost fierce loyalty to our American manufacturers that prevented me from buying a foreign-made automobile.

My decision to purchase a new car came in the summer, but I delayed until September when the new cars came out so I would be in a better bargaining position when dealers were clearing out their present models.

I went to the library and read the motor magazines and the consumer's reports and became quite knowledgeable about what was going on in the car field. I learned that it is considered unwise to purchase a model that is going to be discontinued next year or that will be drastically changed in appearance.

In looking at the money I paid out on repairs for my Cadillac I realized I was paying for a new car whether I bought one or not, so if you can afford a new car they are a better choice for the single woman.

It is important to study the owner's manual and to make sure the oil is changed regularly and the tires are rotated and kept with the proper pressure in them.

Some women find it beneficial to take courses in automobile mechanics which are offered for a nominal fee (far less than one garage bill!) in evening school classes in local high schools. Frankly, considering the high cost of automobile maintenance it might not be a bad idea.

"Do you really think God cares about what kind of a car you drive?" a skeptical friend asked me. I most emphatically do. I believe it is of special importance to him and that he can guide us when we turn to him and depend upon him to do so. I believe that he led me to my present car which has doors that are not too heavy for my arthritic hands to open, just as he led me to that Cadillac for the purpose of allowing my back injury to heal.

LET NO CIRCUMSTANCE DESTROY MY JOY TODAY

> nor happening—
> It is the music of the universe
> angel-song
> to which I am antiphony
>   No tyrant-wind
>   rebel from storm at sea
>   has a right to shred-sail my cloak
>   with fear, anxiety.
> These chords that spell out
> laughter, love are not
> earth-made, but rather
> know the harmony

of heavenly things like star
and cloud and sun
  In this aria
  the day comes dressed
  and fully clothed.
Let nothing, Lord, destroy my song.

19

About that Three-Letter Word

"Don't ever get married for sex — it never works!" This advice was given by my son's track coach when he was in college. The fact that the words were relayed to me proves how much the word *sex* has changed in meaning from my generation to my son's generation.

My mother's advice to me was limited to the reading of a book given me by our neighbor, a retired minister. I had gone to his barn to watch him milk his cow and the sight of a bunch of newborn kittens in the barn raised lots of questions in my seven-year-old head. "Where do kittens come from, Mr. Ashby? And where does everything come from? Where do babies come from?"

Mother read the book to us after tucking us in for the night. My sister fell asleep at the end of the first page. My five-year-old brother only lasted through the birds. But I was determined to stick it out and satisfy my curiosity. The one paragraph about babies was very delicately-stated.

This ended the conversation between my mother and me except for an explanation about "becoming a woman" when I was 12. On that occasion my mother explained the difficulty that her mid-Victorian mother had had in telling her that her "periods" had not started because she had sat on a nail.

I remember no other spoken advice from family members except for a dear aunt who once said to me: "Hasn't anyone ever told you you should never get too close to a boy?" I didn't answer her for I didn't know what to say.

The evils of sex outside of marriage were hammered into my young mind so it was no problem at all for me to remain a virgin until my wedding night.

I am in no way an authority on the subject, but I realize sex is a very real part of the problem among women living alone. Sex can be a very beautiful part of the marriage, and that is what God intended it to be. But he never intended sex for the sake of sex.

God sanctioned sex as a bond between the married, and when it occurs in any other context, the deviation leaves emotional scars. It is an Esau-pottage experience from which those who indulge suffer for years and may never fully recover.

One friend who is living alone confided to me she was seeing a man she had known for several months. They both rode the same commuter train into the city where they worked.

"Oh, are you really considering marrying again?" I asked.

"Of course not," she replied. "He already has a wife back in Greece."

I refused to believe the friendship was anything but platonic for I would not let myself believe she could lower her standards. I realized however that her extreme loneliness was a temptation and continued to call and see her. It was not long until she told me, "I am not seeing him anymore — that 'stuff' is not for me!"

If you were to believe much of the great volume of material that is being written by highly educated, but highly unwise, marriage counsellors, psychologists, doctors, and book opportunists, you could easily be persuaded that it is not normal to live without sex and that you should find a sex partner.

No more erroneous advice could be expounded. Losing a mate does not change old mores. They are still basic to health and happiness and the well-being of both the individual and society.

How the sex mongers try to deceive us into believing their falsehoods! Their standards would turn every home into a brothel. The teachings of the Scriptures are just as necessary to the preservation of life now as they were when written thousands of years ago.

In his inaugural address President Carter said "We must adjust to changing times, but hold to the old principles." These wise words can very well be applied to sex.

I am glad for the new freedom that brings sex out of the dark closet. I am glad my son could come home from college and share with me his coach's advice and that I can talk freely with my daughters on the subject. It is out in the open where it should be. I regret, however, the disproportionate emphasis that society has placed on it. With every freedom comes new responsibility, and herein we are failing drastically. Though important, sex is only a small part of the man/woman relationship.

For years you have lived under the safe umbrella of your husband's presence. You have been sheltered from the onslaughts of the new sexual freedom by your marriage. Now your marriage is over and the protective umbrella is gone, and you find yourself holding only the metal skeleton of the umbrella in your hand. You find you must reassess your mores, your standards. Are you going to be unduly pressured by the free sex all around you or are you wisely going to find that the laws against adultery and fornication were given by a loving God for your protection?

Shakespeare wrote, "Experience is a dear school, but fools will learn in no other." After the wholesomeness of a meaningful marriage relationship you will find an affair can bring no deep satisfaction. Sex out of marriage is definitely a matter of buying a mess of pottage in exchange for the birthright of self-esteem and honor.

"Men do not want platonic relationships — they are looking only for sex!" one woman complained bitterly. She was looking for friends in the wrong places and finding the wrong kind of friends. There are still men who are yearning for meaningful relationships within the orthodox circle of biblical laws and precepts. However, such men are not to be found in a tavern, hotel lobby, by the dating computer, or through advertisements in substandard journalistic newspapers. They may still be found in churches and proper organizations. But even then one should employ more care and consideration than one does in selecting a hat.

In the nursing home where life interests are reduced to a bare minimum, it is noticeable how important and blown completely out of proportion becomes the daily evacuation of the bowels. How sad when life is reduced to such an infinitely small sphere of interest and conversation. Sex, too, has been blown out of proportion in size and place. Why? Because the more vital and captivating facts of life have been allowed to shrivel, shrink, and disappear until all that remains is a vacuum.

Admittedly, the younger widow will have more of a problem in this area usually than the older one whose sexual needs in most instances have diminished with the years.

One of the tragedies of living in some retirement areas is the lack of meaningful and productive activity available for the residents.

One of the retirement centers here in Florida is doing something about the boredom that often accompanies retirement. The women have formed a musical group, the "Ko-Ko-Mo Kuties." They meet once a week for practice and then give light musical programs in the area with proceeds going to needy families. In one year they raised over $2400. They have found aim and purpose for their lives — and have a very good time doing it.

Often when life is reduced to condominium living the single woman finds herself with nothing to do but attend 10 A.M. cocktail parties and spend the day "nipping" on the bottle beside the pool. She has nothing better to do than to get a tan and flirt with someone else's husband. This is tragic.

Sublimation of the sex drive is most difficult under such living conditions, and it is no wonder that so many widows end up alcoholics if not inmates of mental institutions.

There is a wonderful world around us to be explored and enjoyed. There are many physical activities such as tennis, bicycling, square dancing, golf, hiking that help to take care of sexual needs and to produce physical stamina.

It is beneficial and advisable to discuss your sexual adjustment with your doctor, and you may find he will reduce or even withdraw any hormone he may have prescribed for you in the past. Many women of middle age and older are given prescriptions by their doctors for estrogen in order to prevent osteoporosis of the bone, hypertension, "hot flashes," and other problems of aging. This hormone has a definite effect upon sexual desire and if you have been on such a prescription it is quite possible your physician may need to diminish your dosage now that you are a widow.

The mind does control the body, although often in this generation it would seem the other way around. Therefore it is important that you fill your mind with inspirational reading and the old classics.

Recently I met a widow in her 80s. I could not help but wonder what gave her such a zest for living. Then I discovered she was a great reader—always read in bed at night and was presently absorbed in a book she found fascinating about a Stone-Age tribe living in a remote Philippines jungle. Her eyes sparkled as she told me some of the living conditions of this primitive people. Reading had kept her alive and vital! "There is no frigate like a book to take us lands away," wrote Emily Dickinson. It is important, however, to choose your reading material discreetly and avoid the lurid sex novels.

I do not advocate the crass method of telling a man immediately upon introduction that you are not interested in sex and that if that is what he has in mind to forget it. I mention this because only recently I heard of a new widow who makes such pronouncements upon meeting men. What an insult this would be to any man seeking a platonic friendship with her.

You may have to think back a good number of years, but you surely can remember how you "managed" such situations when you were dating. But manage them you did — and manage them you still can.

I can hear the feminists screaming as I write this, but speaking of women's rights — hasn't the woman always had the upper hand where sex is concerned? Like they always used to say: "A boy will go as far as a girl will let him." An intelligent woman has always been able to hold the reins in a man/woman relationship. She chooses whom she will marry and whom she will or will not sleep with. You do not have to subscribe to the theory that "you cannot live without sex." You most assuredly can.

The violation of any of God's laws brings sorrow, separation, and poverty. It is well that we have progressed far from the wearing of scarlet letters, but we cannot escape the invisible letter that burns itself into the heart after such a violation. Only the blood of Jesus Christ can remove it — and even then, in your memory, it can burn and coil like the serpent who fathered it.

We might add to the words of my son's track coach: "Don't form any relationship for sex — it will never work." Not without bringing eventually great unhappiness and guilt feelings into your life. Put your sex life on the altar and accept God's grace to live in continence and communion with him.

In her book, *After the Flowers Are Gone*, Bea Decker has this important paragraph: "The sex drive is a powerful force. The sudden loss of an outlet in marriage creates a difficult readjustment. But there is another three-letter word which is even more powerful, G-O-D."

A close relationship with God is the only way to control sex and its counterpart, loneliness. Without him the widow is subject to falling into the traps of alcoholism, drugs, compulsive spending, tavern living, illicit relationships, TV addiction, or a tragic, rushed-into, unwise second marriage.

In Job 29:13 we read "and I caused the widow's heart to sing for joy." The widow can find joy in serving God in many avenues of service that surround her. No longer is she restrained by the needs of her husband. She is free to come and go as she will.

20

In the Wake
of Divorce

The hurricane lashed violently all through the dark night. Morning dawned with gray weepy skies, its somber light revealing the devastation of the preceding hours. The house was razed to the ground. Rubbish and debris were scattered everywhere — in the bushes, trees, and over the walkways. The occupants while still living suffered untold injuries, contusions, abrasions, fractures. An array of rescue squads and relief units moved in quickly to offer the family many forms of help — medical help for bodily injuries, temporary shelter, food and clothing, until their home could be cleared of debris and new housing built.

The destructive force we know as divorce is just as devastating to a family, although the injuries are seldom visible to the naked eye. The devastation is emotional and internal, but just as real as that in the wake of the hurricane.

Eric, a first-grader, was an unusually bright and happy child. Every morning he greeted his teacher with, "Hi. Will you be my buddy today?" His classmates loved his outgoing personality and he was a favorite in choosing games. But quite suddenly his personality underwent a drastic change. His skip was replaced by slow-moving steps. He failed to greet teacher and classmates. He sat in his seat listlessly staring out the window. His teacher was baffled by this change in behavior. She inquired about him from other teachers in the school and then called his mother and father.

It was then she found the hurricane had struck.

One afternoon she asked Eric to stay after class. She put the unhappy child on her lap and asked him what the matter was. Tears streamed down the little face but he could not answer. Wisely the teacher told him, "Eric, sometimes grownups have trouble getting along with each other. Your daddy didn't leave home because he doesn't love you. He still loves you and you will see him again. It is just that your parents have decided not to live together anymore. There are other children in this class whose fathers no longer live in the same house. Johnny's daddy moved out last year. . .and Missy's daddy doesn't live at her house anymore either. You must not think that just because he has gone to live some place else your daddy doesn't love you anymore!"

The next morning the child returned to school with some of the burden lifted. He came up to her desk and said, "Mrs. Bell, will you be my buddy today?"

Shortly after this episode the teacher resigned from her position and, for Eric's sake, she said she was glad the replacement was a man. He came several days to observe the class before she left. On the last day she was there she saw Eric come in all smiles as he skipped up to the new teacher and asked, "Will you be my buddy today?" Perhaps this incident points out the need for male substitutes in the lives of children whose parents are divorced.

Unfortunately, it will not be so easy to find a substitute for Eric's mother.

When a young woman named Rachel legally severed the bonds from her tragic first marriage it became a national scandal—a scandal that did not lose its fury when she married one Andrew Jackson who soon became President of the United States.

The stigma of her divorce was to follow her into high governmental circles and ostracize her from some Washingtonian society, despite the fact that she was the First Lady. The mental harassment she suffered was no doubt partly responsible for her illness and subsequent early grave.

No matter how justifiable a divorce may be, and even though the stigma has greatly diminished since Rachel Jackson's day, it still has ways of subtly attaching itself to the divorcee. Some schools for higher education will not accept divorced students. Some companies slip the divorcee's name to the bottom of their employment list. Some churches will not take divorcee's into their membership.

The divorcee — in addition to suffering what must be devastating feelings of rejection — must also suffer the rejection of various segments of society.

When there are children caught in the hurricane along with herself the dilemma is even more difficult to solve. Often the courts award the father visiting time. This is an added pressure if she feels he is unfit to be a proper father to her children.

One divorcee had the problem of her ex-husband sharing his marijuana with her children, ages five and seven.

She solved it by moving as far away from him as she could.

My friend Lorraine gave birth to her fifth child, a nine-pound boy. In a family of three girls and one boy he was a most welcome addition to balance out the sexes. The children welcomed home their new brother with gifts of red and blue construction paper which they hung above his crib. The baby's father gave quite another kind of gift for his infant son — a divorce petition he handed his wife a day or so after she returned home.

Lorraine was devastated. She had trusted in him blindly. His late nights at the shop had been more and more frequent during her pregnancy but she had been involved with the needs of her four children and had not had time to wonder whether or not he was seeing another woman.

For the most part Lorraine ostracized herself from society after the divorce. She suffered from a sense of failure and rejection. Her visits to church were only sporadic and failed to give her the spiritual lift she desperately needed.

Two children were born to her ex-husband's new marriage. Soon, however, he began coming to his first family for more and more frequent visits. He confided in Lorraine how unhappy he was in his new marriage. He had married an older woman, already twice-divorced, who worked in his office.

Inwardly, Lorraine could not keep from gloating over the way his marriage was working. But when he finally asked her if she would consider taking him back if he divorced his new wife, she said no. She realized marriage must be built on trust and faith and these she would never be able to feel towards him again.

Molly was a delightful girl of Irish descent who married young and had eight children. The strain of caring for their needs was apparently more than their marriage could handle. Her husband turned to alcohol for escape and soon became an alcoholic.

On several occasions Molly's drunken husband beat her and some of the children. Molly began to give serious thought to divorce, but did nothing about it until a later time when, after two weeks in the hospital, she came home to find he had moved one of his girl friends into the house during her absence.

Although thoroughly justified, the divorce was a deeply traumatic experience. Molly moved out of the house and into an apartment with the three younger children. She enrolled the two girls in a nearby school where they were very unhappy. After three days she came home from her work to find her husband had come after the girls, taken them with him, and enrolled them in their old school where they could be with their friends.

Peers are important to children, and because of their enrollment in their old school, the girls now spend the week in their father's home and return to Molly's apartment on the weekends. Though contrary to court order, this is where the girls have chosen to remain. Their father drinks heavily and entertains other women in his apartment. Molly worries that his wanton lifestyle will have a bad effect upon her daughters, but she has almost no control over what takes place in his life now.

It is better in most instances for the divorce to be a complete break, for this offers both parties a greater chance for healing the wounds and starting over. This is easier to do, of course, when children are not involved. However, children from a broken home are much bet-

ter off than children caught in a home in the process of
breaking up.

For the divorcee healing can take place more rapidly if
she can close the door to the past firmly and ask God's
forgiveness for whatever bitterness she may still be holding in her heart. The Holy Spirit can pour his healing oil
upon her wounds and restore her to wholesomeness once
again.

Employment can be a great help for the woman who
needs to be back in the mainstream of society once again.
It can make her feel independent so she can cut all ties to
her unhappy past. Although remarriage can sometimes
turn out happily, that is extremely rare.

Years ago I worked with a young woman whose parents had married, divorced, and remarried several times.
After one of the divorces I heard the girl say how glad she
was they were divorced again. I questioned her about her
feelings and she said, "Oh, they just can't get along when
they are married, but they get along fine when they are
divorced."

It seemed he continued to eat meals with the family
and perhaps kept a room in the house.

The emotional scars from dissolving a relationship run
very deep and the adjustments are perhaps even more
difficult than for the woman severing a legal marriage. In
a common-law marriage a woman gets very little, if any,
understanding from her friends or society itself.

A praying spiritual friend can prove most helpful to the
divorcee. Someone who can hear her out while she spills
out the pent-up feelings of bitterness and resentment.
Someone who can pray with her that the Holy Spirit will
heal her transgressions and cover them with the precious
blood of the Lamb.

Marriage may or may not be made in heaven. Some very definitely are. The origin of others may be seriously in doubt. Divorce comes out of the pit — even when it seems like the only route to take.

Joe Bayly once wrote, "Hatred made a wound, but Love saw that there were no scars." God can see to it that emotional scars are healed — that there remains no bitterness, no resentment, no hatred or self-pity. Consider the past a closed chapter in your life. Realize that the chapters ahead may be more exciting and beautiful if you will let them be. But this cannot happen if you are going to dwell in the past and keep rereading the old worn pages. It will do you no good to keep thinking, "if I had only done this or that." There are had-onlys in all our lives but they must be yielded to the Spirit of God.

21

Marry Again?

When Catherine Hudson was killed in an automobile accident in California, her husband Paul was grief-stricken.

His first impulse, when he saw his wife's body thrown under the truck, was to throw himself after her. His grief was further intensified by the knowledge that she had only been a passenger; he was driving the car.

The two children — an eight-year-old girl and a two-year-old boy — required extensive surgery. The boy suffered the beginnings of an emotional psychosis that would plague him the rest of his life.

Returning to Illinois, Paul buried his wife and tried to make a home for his children. An aunt kept house for several weeks, and she was followed by a rapid succession of housekeepers. One fell in love with Paul. Another became ill with a terminal illness.

Each housekeeper was a mother-figure for little Larry and he suffered when each departed. By the time he was eight he had lost four "mothers." The emotional damage was irreparable.

Paul tried to forget his grief, at first, by throwing himself into club activities. This frustrated his children because they in a way had now lost not only their mother but part of their father, too.

Five years later, Paul became attracted to one of Larry's teachers. They developed a fine relationship and were married.

Everything ran smoothly for a time in the Hudson home. Daughter Linda, now 14, began to show the first signs of maladjustment. She had been the lady of the house for six years and did not like being "upstaged." However, the birth of little Timmy brought Linda much joy and helped her forget her complaints.

Larry's reaction to Timmy, however, was more complicated. He resented the newcomer. The birth of a second boy to Paul and Evelyn only accentuated the situation.

Evelyn was an unusually fine woman and highly skilled in the managing of children in her classes. Unfortunately Larry's problems ran too deep. He suffered from angry violent outbursts which were usually directed at Timmy. On one occasion Larry hurled a chair at Timmy. He missed and it went through a dining-room window.

In the interests of safety for the smaller boys, Larry could no longer stay at home. He was sent to the home of a Christian psychiatrist who was a friend of Paul's.

Linda, too, suffered eventually from emotional problems. She rebelled at the idea of going to a Christian college and chose a secular campus, fell in love with a young man of whom her father did not approve, and eventually married another young man whose intellectual capacities were below hers. She had four children who chose to live with their father when the divorce was finalized.

Today Linda lives alone in a small city apartment, emotionally ill and unable to cope with the circumstances.

Larry married a lovely Christian teacher, but that marriage eventually failed, too. Even a slight disagreement would trigger dangerous outbursts of violence on his part.

The products of broken homes can be seen everywhere in our country today. When a parent is left without a mate he or she needs to look at the situation pragmatically and seek the Lord's guidance in providing a suitable mate and parent for their children.

When there is no father in the home, it is unfortunate for children's lives to be dominated by women. To help the single mother, churches often provide stand-in father programs that can be of real value to the fatherless child.

As an example, Paul Hudson's home situation might have been somewhat easier had he adjusted more quickly to his wife's death and married when his children were younger. Five years was apparently too long.

Paul the Apostle reminded the widow to "remain even as I," and to continue to serve the Lord. Some may feel that Paul's ideas were chauvinistic, but no doubt he saw the difficulties in adjusting to a second marriage. The problems are manifold and they increase with the age of the people involved.

You have probably seen unhappy second marriages where the persons made constant verbal references to their first mates. A deep-seated loyalty to the first mate sometimes makes it impossible to make the necessary adjustments needed for the second marriage to succeed. Time has a way of erasing the faults of the deceased so that by comparison the present wife or husband can indeed come out on the short end.

A second marriage must be far more than companionship. Love must be the primary motive in order for two people to live together in harmony. This must be a love that is "willing to do anything to help and unwilling to do anything to hinder."

If you know in your heart that there could never be another love in your life then be honest with yourself and those around you.

For the most part career women may have an easier time adjusting to widowhood because they have already carved out a world of their own into which their husbands never intruded.

If you feel strongly that you would like to marry again, keep this matter to yourself. There are subtler things you can do to realize your goal than to broadcast it by word and action among the people you meet.

How are you going to meet eligible men? This is indeed a problem, for the number of bachelors and widowers in this country is very small.

One of the rules in fishing is to go where the fish are. To meet eligible Christian men is to go where they are. Attend church and church social functions. Bible conferences are another excellent place to meet fine Christian men.

Consider your situation prayerfully for it is important that you be divinely led to a second mate. Such a marriage must be God's will — not your will — for your life. Otherwise, the grief of a second unhappy union could exceed that which accompanied the loss of your first mate.

In the first marriage you were young and able to adjust quite readily to your husband's food likes and dislikes. Yours were in a formative stage, and if he disliked liver it was not hard to decide not to cook liver. If he wanted cornbread at every meal you didn't find this hard to adjust to, either.

But by now your eating patterns have been established. The 4 P.M. tea hour that you have been accustomed to may seem entirely unnecessary to your second mate. This is only a trivial example, but it is the trivial things that grow into a mountain whose summit bears the flag "incompatible."

Mary Masters has a peculiar problem. Her husband retires at 6 P.M. every night and then arises for a large breakfast at 2 or 3 in the morning.

She cannot go to sleep that early, and after retiring at 10 or 11 does not want to arise at 2 A.M. for bacon, eggs, and potatoes!

So they breakfast alone, although they do get together for lunch and early supper. Mary complains to her neighbors that in many ways she is a widow without really being one. Where their social life is concerned, she is right, because he never wants to go any place in the evening and if she invites friends over she will have to entertain them alone. He is invariably asleep.

They have been married many years, however, and their differences are not new to one another. They have worked out a compatibility of sorts. But if they had just married just to have a mate, his early bedtime and 2 A.M. breakfasting could well have driven her up the wall.

This is an extreme case, but it does serve to illustrate some of the problems that may exist in a second marriage.

Ann Boswell's happy first marriage ended with her husband's death. It was a shattering experience and her entire life focused upon finding a man to fill the void her husband had left.

She met a wealthy banker whose wife had just died, and a hasty marriage was the result. She was shocked to find him spend their wedding night with a bottle of liquor.

She had had no idea he was an alcoholic. She put up with this for two years, but the lovely home he provided meant nothing in light of his drinking. He was constantly pointing out her faults and comparing her to his first wife.

If Ann had not been in such a hurry to remarry she might have considered whether or not he had indeed gotten over his first marriage and his love for his first wife. She might also have found out about his drinking. The traumatic experience that followed, intensified by the divorce that resulted from it, was not worth the hurry.

There are many things that are far worse than living alone. Whether you marry or not, it is important that you become an interesting person. You will enjoy yourself much more with a mind full of interesting thoughts than if you have made no effort in self-improvement. You will also become more interesting to members of the opposite sex.

Lest in my desire to caution you about the possible hazards involved in a second marriage I should appear too negative about the idea, let me include in this chapter the story of two women who have had very happy second marriages.

Clover Boldt, a fine poet with married children, lost

her husband and moved to southern Florida. She purchased a home from a widower who was moving to Connecticut. As she watched him leave she jokingly called out, "Well if you miss your home too much, come back and I will rent you the best room in the house!"

The following February Mr. Baird decided he could not stand the arctic New England winter and found his way back to Florida.

Clover met him at the door and was happy to see him, for she needed to know where the septic tank was located.

To make a long story short, Clover Boldt became Clover Baird. Mr. Baird did move back into his former home — rent-free!

A second woman had a story-book romance. She took a round-the-world cruise with a couple of old friends. The first night of the cruise the couple introduced her to a widower friend of theirs who was also on the tour.

The next day, in one of the ports, these two found themselves deserted by their married friends so they saw the sights together. They found that they had many things in common, and before long when they went sightseeing in another port they stopped at a jewelry store where he bought her an emerald engagement ring.

They planned to be married in Hong Kong but decided to be married "secretly" in the United States Embassy Office in Cape Town, South Africa. Their secret was soon out and a celebration of the event became part of the ship's entertainment. It is a very happy marriage for which the bride gives this reason: "We believed the Lord brought us together — and so we were married!"

That's the answer to the question, "Marry again?" If the Lord brings you together, get married!

22

Words Fitly Spoken

"Buck up, now! You'll make it! You'll get married again!"

They were the summary of an hour's brash attempt to comfort a new widow by a young woman who could not have said more wrong things if she had been hired to say them.

Following several hours' illness, Signe's husband had died of a massive coronary on Sunday morning. After a memorial service in a West Palm Beach funeral home on Monday (attended by all of the residents of Monet Acres), on Tuesday the casket was placed on the plane, and suffering from both shock and grief, Signe accompanied her beloved's body back to Illinois for first a visitation, and then a funeral and burial on Wednesday. I had offered to travel with her for moral support.

Our seat companion was young—not so much in years as in the ways of grief. It was obvious she had never known more than the loss of a dog. After we had introduced ourselves, she immediately asked, "Are you married?" Signe, one of the most charming and gracious women I know, explained with difficulty that her husband had just died and we were taking his body back to Illinois to be buried.

We had made the mistake of introducing ourselves to Mrs. Brash, and had I dreamed what we were letting ourselves in for, I would have been politely rude and neglected the introductions.

"This happens every day. . ." she exclaimed in her gutteral voice and proceeded to tell us of a woman in her condominium whose husband had also died and "might even be on this same plane."

It does happen every day, but it only happened once in Signe's 55 years of an intrinsically happy marriage.

"There is no hell. . .I'm a Catholic, but they can't make me believe in hell. . .so you can know your husband is not in hell. . .purgatory, maybe, but never hell."

Then followed a tirade of self-imposed theological exposition on why she did not believe a loving God would ever send anyone to hell.

"Signe is a Presbyterian. . ." I tried unsuccessfully to shut her up.

"You're attractive. . ." she yelled at Signe who was seated by the window, "it'll be no time until you'll be married again."

At this Signe lost her composure and the tears gushed down her cheeks.

"No, you don't understand," I admonished Mrs. Brash, "Signe has been married for over 50 years and the very thought of a remarriage is very painful." It failed to restrain our insensitive seatmate.

"Oh, you don't begin to look your age. You'll find someone. There are lots of widowers around everywhere. And besides you know, your last years are the easiest in life. . ." she said, from the mountain of wisdom accumulated in her some 20 or 30 years.

On and on she rattled, ruthlessly overlooking any and all proprieties. Greatly disturbed by her raucous intonations, I changed the subject time after time only to have her rush headlong with the football of conversation into the end zones where angels were fearing to tread.

Finally, I turned toward the window and leaned forward—an effort to protect Signe from our incredible companion by engaging her in conversation on the scenery and landscape. The presence of Mrs. Brash made me glad for one thing—my decision to accompany my friend on her sad journey.

On arriving home, when I told my son about the episode, he charitably commented, "Well, you know, I find it very hard to know what to say when someone has died."

C. S. Lewis in his *A Grief Observed* gives an account of his wife's long illness, her death from cancer, and the agony of loneliness and grief following her burial. He comments at length on the way people he knew avoided him. It is indeed difficult to know what to say to a bereaved person. Do you ignore the death, act as if nothing has happened although you know the survivor's world has split apart? Do you discuss the weather? The latest crisis in the world? The political scene? Men are especially at a loss for words in the face of such delicate matters. But better a complete void of expression than a Mrs. Brash with her lexicon of crude advice.

You who have recently lost your mate have experienced all of the peculiar attempts of your friends and acquaintances to offer condolence. You are aware of what either shattered the fragile teacups of your ears or brought you comfort and support. The phone call that said, "You are very much on my mind in these days and I just want you to know I am praying for you."

Or the whispered words at the funeral home, "God will see you through."

"God knows all about it and He will work everything out for you. You can trust Him through it all."

"My heart aches for you, Mary. I want to help you in any way I can."

"I know this must be terribly difficult for you for I know how much you and Howard meant to each other."

At the height of my husband's illness, one friend pressed an envelope into my hand at the hospital with the simple words on it, "the clouds we dread so much are full of mercy." I still carry it in one of my purses and whenever I read it, the well meaning of her sympathy is mine again.

Had Mrs. Brash had any sensitivity in her make-up she would have said something like, "I am so very sorry to hear about it. . .and I shall remember you in my prayers." The simple expression would have brought comfort, but the wild tirade she poured out was unbelievably in poor taste—and all we could tell ourselves afterwards was, "Well, she meant all right."

But it is not enough to mean all right. If ever discretion is important it is when there is a serious illness or a death. *The greatest privilege we have in life is to be able to serve someone in the moment of their need.*

When her husband died, there were many needs in Signe's life. One I could meet by choosing to return to Chicago with her on the same plane. There was another small token of my sympathy—a poem I had written in memory of her husband. A simple poem, for he was a simple, kind hearted man, a retired farmer. Although I could not attend the funeral service, the little poem, read by the minister, in a way served to take my place and I knew it brought comfort to the hearts of the bereaved.

In big city living so many of the amenities that make life in a small town meaningful are fast disappearing. Often the city dweller goes through the loss of a child, or mate, without the neighbors in the apartment building even being aware of the death. Such a void of concern and expressions of love and sympathy is heart breaking.

My childhood was spent in a small community centered around my home church. I well remember the sympathy and love that found their way to our door when my father died in the form of casseroles, warm breads, cakes as well as flowers. Although we lived in Chicago for eight years before we moved to the suburban town we now live in, I never got used to "big city indifference."

Sometimes the more important the position a man holds the more it widens the void around him and his family when grief enters. When the president of the school in Chicago in which my husband taught died soon after my husband had become a member of the faculty, I simply followed my small-town upbringing and took a casserole and a book of consolation to his widow. The president had died on the West Coast and funeral arrangements included a memorial service at the school in Chicago and then another cross-country trip, by train, for his widow to New York state for the burial.

Afterwards she told me, "You will never know what your coming meant to me that day. It was such a long hard journey and I took your book with me and read it on the way." What a little thing for me to do—and yet I knew it had given her comfort in her great need.

Perhaps you do not know the bereaved very well, but the need is there—and the privilege is also there for you to serve. Don't let the big city crowd out your natural aptitude for conveying kindness. Think of something special to do. A plate of cookies. A casserole. A salad. A book of poetry. A house plant. Something that says, "Even though this is an inhospitable world, I want you to know I care." An envelope pressed into a hand. . .apples of gold in pictures of silver. . .

You cannot know how much such a kind expression can mean to someone in the depths of grief. . .unless you have been bereaved and the recipient of such love.

You as a widow do know what grief is all about. . .and you know instinctively what words should be said and what should be left unspoken.

Never would you hurt someone who has just lost her mate with the words "Oh, you will marry again!" You know that such words are like a hot searing knife that burn and burn. A woman who has lost her husband cannot bear the thought of anyone trying to take his place. To hint at such a possibility can only bring her agony of soul.

You as a widow are in the position to be able "to comfort others with the comfort wherein you yourself have been comforted."

On the plane back to Wheaton, Signe confided, "I am so grateful God has taken Howard home before me. I never wanted him to be left alone without me to look after him." There was no self-pity in her voice. She knew God's choice in her life was the right one and she faced the funeral and the days ahead confident in the God whom she believed had every right to call His child home—in His time. In such acceptance, her soul found serenity and peace. She was a living example of the motto:

"Give me the SERENITY to accept what I cannot change, the COURAGE to change what I cannot accept, and the WISDOM to know the difference."

There are thousands of women, many in your acquaintance, who have never known a happy marriage, nor have they loved and been loved. You have known the ultimate in human relationships. You have loved and been loved. Your widowhood is not the tragedy some would make it appear even though you may be feeling now that you have a very high price to pay for the love you knew. True, you have—but it was worth it!

You have had a rich and fulfilling life. You know how to give the warm embrace, the love-kiss on the cheek, the firm handclasp, the soft pats on the shoulder that often say more than words can convey.

You can speak gently as you would comfort a sobbing child. You know when a whisper, or a touch of the hand, can convey the comfort that is so needed. You have experienced the gentle dove of the Holy Spirit's own comforting voice. You now know how to pass that gentleness along to the grief stricken and the lonely. God wants you to be his messenger with his healing balm in your touch and his loving kindness in your voice.

Not only is the week of the funeral important to exercise such means of comfort, but in the months ahead, your widowed friend is going to need your help in making her most difficult adjustments back into the world of the living.

When after the trip with Signe I returned to my home in Wheaton I found the water pipes in the street were frozen solid. There was no water. . .for drinking. . .for brushing teeth. . .for bathing. . .nor for washing clothes. A friend took my clothes home to launder. Another brought me two plastic gallons of water. A neighbor lent me a long garden hose attached to his outside spigot. One friend brought me a singular gift. . .four small chocolate bars. She knew I was on a diet. She also knew I needed some "consolation food." It took the city four days to restore my water because the frost extended far below the water pipes, but in the meantime the small considerations of my friends greatly helped me in living alone in a house without water.

I also found that one of the women in my Bible club had lost her husband while I was away. His death followed a long illness and hospitalization in an institution some miles from her home. Daily visits took time from her household tasks and his death found her house in disarray with relatives expected for the funeral. Three of the women in our Bible study helped her clean her house. They were meeting the expediency of her need. Two of them followed through on arrangements for a luncheon to be served at the church after the funeral. The expressions of love did much to sustain her through the trying ordeal. She was, in fact, so impressed by the love extended to her by the church that on the Sunday following the funeral she went forward on a confession of faith and became a member. She is a new Christian and had never had a church affiliation.

How important it is for the Body of Christ to minister to members of his Body during periods of need. We are admonished to look after the household of God *before* we go into the byways and hedges.

Edith Schaeffer in her book, *A Way of Seeing*, writes "seeking first *the kingdom of God* does not mean a comfortable giving of a couple of hours a week in church, or writing a check to a 'cause,' but rather an openness, a sensitiveness to be led by the Lord in ways that interrupt the putting of our own way or our own interests first. We must allow his interruptions to come first, before our own preferred schedule." The phone call from a lonely widow, the visitor who appears at an inconvenient time at the door; an impression (which may be from the Lord) to stop by to see someone or other who may be in desperate need of our visit.

A prestigious home can turn into a fortress that prevents the entrance of any form of condolence when there is a death in the family. This was the case when Martha Hartley's husband James passed away. Although they had been church members for many years and had often opened their home to church groups for social functions, no one came near to express sympathy or to bring offerings of food or flowers. The widow's loneliness was doubly emphasized because the couple had no children and she found herself without the support of friends or family. His business associates sent floral pieces to the funeral home, but overlooked the importance of remembering the widow in more personal ways. There is something about wealth and position that has a tendency to build walls and shut those-that-have in and those-that-have-not out. Often tragedy cannot break down social barriers, and the most lonely widows of all often are those who are isolated in wealthy mansions with maybe only the solace of a hired maid or the condolence of a yard man when grief enters the massive front door.

Poverty has its advantages in that it is easier to express kindness where there is material lack or need evident than when affluence is present. Then the attitude may be, "What could I possibly buy her or take her that she does not already have?" It is easy to forget that it is not the gift that counts, but the thoughtful concern it expresses on the part of the giver. The wealthy widow may have to endure her grief alone without any or very few expressions of sympathy because her acquaintances and friends feel constrained by a social barrier, either real or imagined, as the case may be.

Letter writing can add dimensions to your life and serve as a ministry to those to whom you write. My husband was an avid mail watcher. As soon as he heard the clang of the mail box opening, it would signal him to the door and he eagerly brought in the mail. There could be a number of pieces, but he would sometimes say, "There is nothing today." He meant, of course, nothing personal. Never a letter writer himself (except during the months we were engaged!) he always looked for letters from friends, family and former students. Letter writing was not his avocation—it fell to me. His family would never have heard from us had I not written. But still he expectantly looked for the mail.

Probably you found the same to be true. I am glad now I was the letter writer for it is a habit that adds greatly to the pleasure of the day now that I am alone. Today, I received a letter from a friend in which her husband, a busy lawyer, had tucked a handwritten note. I especially appreciate this type of thoughtfulness now that I am alone. Write a letter today to someone who may be lonelier than you are. I shall write to Jane, a former member of my Bible club who has moved away from all of her much-loved friends to a beautiful retirement home her husband built in the mountains of Tennessee. Although her home is such as should afford much happiness, she has many serious problems: a daughter who is obese, a misfit in society and has tried to commit suicide, an aged mother who has nearly died several times in the past year, and a husband whose retirement means riding a tractor and who either cannot or will not communicate with her in any way. For a woman used to many friends in her life this new move to a far country has proved to be difficult. Yes, her loneliness is greater than my own. There is no one she can laugh and pray with or who will listen to her talk. I am surrounded by warm friends, laughter, and joy—although I am without a man in the house—a woman alone.

In the Cosmos Club in Washington, D.C., at the top of a long winding stairway where the steps are covered in deep royal blue velvet carpeting, there is a hall lined with framed pictures of members on one wall who have been awarded the Pulitzer prize for special achievements. On the opposite wall contained in framed pictures are those members who have been awarded the Nobel prize for peace. I could not help but wonder as I studied the names and faces if their memberships had preceded their awards and honors or if they had been made members after receiving their honors. I was secretly glad that being a Christian does not depend upon any of our achievements or honors. When we are yet nothing, we become members of Christ's body upon his invitation, by accepting his free gift of salvation. We are joint heirs with Christ because of his love for us and because of his divine appointment—not because of our talent or productivity.

In Betty Carlson's book, *No One's Perfect*, she tells about a busy mother with many children who solved her need for solitude in a simple and direct way. When things got beyond her, she would sit down and throw her apron up over her head. The children would quiet down realizing that their mother was praying. For the woman alone, there may be no need of an apron, but there is still a desperate need for a time for communion with God. A Psalm? A poem? A verse of Scripture? Any of these can prove to be as effective as an apron thrown over our heads, separating us from the demands of the living that is going on around us, in order that we may reach out to those who need our ministry.

Do you feel the need of prayer and support in your life? Invite two or three of your friends or neighbors in for a morning Bible club with simple refreshments. God has promised that "where two or three are gathered together in my name, there am I in the midst of them" (Matt. 18:20).

After Bea Decker's husband died suddenly of a heart attack, she took her children and moved from Chicago where they had been living back to her home city in Pennsylvania. There the Lord impressed her with the need to help widows, and she began a self-help group for the newly widowed. She called her organization, THEOS, "They Help Each Other Spiritually."

God has blessed her efforts, and there are THEOS groups in many cities and towns of this country. If you are interested in joining or starting such a group in your area, information may be obtained by writing: Bea Decker, THEOS Foundation, 11609 Frankstown Road,

Pittsburgh, PA 15235. I know of no greater help for the
newly widowed than to become a part of a small caring
Bible study group. Such support can prove invaluable in
your making an adjustment back into reality and finding a
contribution that you can make to society.

I FEEL SO SMALL, LORD

here on my square of sidewalk—
and the world is so big.
      From Your perspective,
      do I look like an ant
      running in and out
      of an ant hill? Vulnerable
      to heel and toe of something
      larger than myself?
Then I remember: You said
"in my image—male and female
made I them." And in Romans
You had Paul write: "Nothing
can separate us from the Love
of God." Neither earthquake
nor famine, nor things present,
nor things to come.
      No Big Foot, nor avalanche
      can stamp me out for I am not
      an ant, nor a mere creature—
      but a person made in your likeness—
      a part of Your Eternity.

23

From a Basket
by the Door

In closing, I wonder have I said in these pages all my heart would say? I have just reread *Gift from the Sea*, one of the most loved books on my book shelf which I reread from time to time. I remember how when I read it first I was impressed by the oyster shell clinging tenaciously to its reef—because I was in that state of my life—working hard to rear a family.

But now that my children are grown I find that it is Anne Morrow Lindbergh's final stage, the Argonauta, with which I now find rapport. The argonauta, named for Jason's fleet on its search for the Golden Fleece, freely floats on the surface of the sea on calm days, and from her cradle shell empties her young into the smooth sea water. She is free to float on the diamond-studded water, in the warming sun, beneath the tropical sky. The argonauta has outgrown her shell and, shedding it, forms a new one, pristine white, more suited to her pristine needs.

Mrs. Lindbergh writes in her chapter on the Argonauta, "Woman must come of age herself. This is the essence of 'coming of age'—to learn how to stand alone. She must learn not to depend on another. . .she must become whole."

Whenever I hear John Donne's often quoted line, "No man is an island," my heart cries, "Every man or woman is an island—alone—surrounded by the great sea of life." There are many experiences we must face alone—for in aloneness are the most important lessons of all life to be learned.

I am by nature a beach comber. I love to walk alone on a beach, see the gulls slide on the airwaves, hear the throb and pulse of the tide, watch the sandpipers hurry before the water without ever getting wet. This past year it has been my good fortune to walk along the shore of both the Atlantic in southern Florida and the cobalt blue Pacific in Seattle and San Francisco. Each time, alone or with them, I share with my grandchildren the simple ecstasy of finding shells. How we delight in new shapes, new colors, and new kinds.

But there is one shell which although I search for it diligently each time I go beach combing, I have never had the pleasure of finding newly tossed up from the water's treasure trove. It is the sand dollar.

In Moclips, Washington, where I visited last summer in an artist-friend's home, built high on a bluff over the Pacific, I had my desire to "find" a sand dollar fulfilled not on the sand itself but in a basket by her door. As I was leaving after a day of unforgettable joy in and around her house, she said to me, "Oh, would you like a sand dollar? Here, in the basket—take one as you go!" It is on my desk in Wheaton, this most mystical of all shells. Each time I look at it, I think of the beautiful sapphire of the ocean and the topaz beaches.